11/12

Student Handbook to Sociology

Socialization

Volume IV

Student Handbook to Sociology

Socialization

Volume IV

LIZ GRAUERHOLZ

ELIZABETH SWART

Facts On File
An Infobase Learning Company

Student Handbook to Sociology: Socialization

Facts On File, Inc.
An Imprint of Infobase Learning
132 West 31st Street
New York NY 10001

Library of Congress Cataloging-in-Publication Data

Student handbook to sociology / Liz Grauerholz, general editor.
    v. cm.
    Includes bibliographical references and index.
    Contents: v. 1. History and theory—v. 2. Research methods—v. 3. Social structure—v. 4. Socialization—v. 5. Stratification and inequality—v. 6. Deviance and crime—v. 7. Social change.
    ISBN 978-0-8160-8314-5 (alk. paper)—ISBN 978-0-8160-8315-2 (v. 1 : alk. paper)—ISBN 978-0-8160-8316-9 (v. 2 : alk. paper)—ISBN 978-0-8160-8317-6 (v. 3 : alk. paper)—ISBN 978-0-8160-8319-0 (v. 4 : alk. paper)—ISBN 978-0-8160-8320-6 (v. 5 : alk. paper)—ISBN 978-0-8160-8321-3 (v. 6 : alk. paper)—ISBN 978-0-8160-8322-0 (v. 7 : alk. paper)
    1. Sociology. I. Grauerholz, Elizabeth, 1958–
    HM585.S796 2012
    301—dc23   2011025983

Facts On File books are available at special discounts when purchased in bulk quantities for businesses, associations, institutions, or sales promotions. Please call our Special Sales Department at (212) 967-8800 or (800) 322-8755.

You can find Facts On File on the World Wide Web at
http://www.infobaselearning.com

Text design and composition by Erika K. Arroyo
Cover printed by Yurchak Printing, Landisville, Pa.
Book printed and bound by Yurchak Printing, Landisville, Pa.
Date Printed: April 2012
Printed in the United States of America

10 9 8 7 6 5 4 3 2 1

This book is printed on acid-free paper.

CONTENTS

FOREWORD

Sociology is the study of social groups that make up institutions, cultures, and societies. It may seem that the individual gets lost or ignored in such an examination, but if we remember that all groups are made up of individuals, we see that the individual is at the heart of sociology. This is nowhere more clear than in the study of socialization. Socialization, as you'll see in this volume, is the process by which individuals become functioning members of the groups and societies to which they belong. Its focus is squarely on the individual, but always with an eye to how she or he is connected to the larger social world.

The study of socialization—the process and outcomes—has been of major interest to sociologists for decades. This is due, in part, to the fact that many of the topics sociologists are interested in, such as gender or self-concept, cannot be fully understood without considering socialization experiences. But there is another important reason why sociologists are so interested in the socialization experience. We recognize that socialization is the means through which individuals are connected to society. After all, we are all born into an existing society, with its norms, institutions, values, and so on. But how do we acquire deep knowledge and understanding of these societal features? The answer is socialization. Socialization is what connects individuals to society at large. Without socialization, there could be no stable society.

The study of socialization also illustrates a fundamental principle of sociology—that everything we do and know is influenced by social factors. Socialization always occurs within a social context, around and with other people. So even though socialization produces very unique individuals, individuals are social products. How each person comes to understand him or herself, and how she or he is understood and perceived by others, is constructed through the socialization process.

In this volume, the authors introduce you to this important sociological concept that has shaped sociologists' understanding of individuals and societies for decades. You will learn what socialization is, how it occurs, and some of its most important outcomes. Later, when you're exploring other sociological topics such as institutions, social change, or crime, you will see how socialization becomes a recurring theme for each. Thus, understanding socialization can help you see the "big picture." It can also provide insight into how you, as an individual, became who and what you are today. Such is one of the key promises of sociology—to help individuals see how their own lives have been shaped by external forces.

—Liz Grauerholz, University of Central Florida

INTRODUCTION

Sociology is the study of human groups—from the small (friendships, partnerships) to the large (societies, institutions). But sociologists never lose sight of what constitutes all groups, no matter how diverse or complex, and that is the *individual*. In this volume, our focus is primary on the individual, but always with an eye toward understanding her or his connection to the larger group. That is, this volume provides an in-depth look at how individuals—me, you, everyone—come to be integral parts of social groups. This is, in fact, the essence of *socialization*.

As we note in the first chapter of this volume, when done well, socialization seems natural and seamless. But sociologists insist that the process by which individuals come to "belong" is not natural, that it doesn't simply happen through some biological or physiological process. Rather, the process that links individuals to social groups is decidedly social. As you read this volume, this point will become clearer. You will see that there is tremendous variation in how people organize their lives. Even social positions that are similar across cultures in terms of their functions (e.g., "wife" or "religious leader") are carried out differently depending upon the historical and cultural contexts in which they occur. And the beauty of it is that how an individual enacts his or her roles will (for the most part) be a good fit with a particular society's or group's needs. It is in this way that socialization helps ensure the smooth functioning of society at large.

But one of the most important outcomes of socialization is not what happens on the broad, societal level, but what occurs at the individual level. That is the development of the self and identity. Part of that sense each of us has of being a unique individual involves basic identities we hold near and dear to ourselves, such as gender or racial identities. These too, as you'll see, are the result of socialization.

In Chapter 1 we explain what is meant by socialization from a sociological perspective, and why it is so important to understanding society. Here we also spell out sociological assumptions about socialization that are revisited throughout the volume. Chapter 2 examines in-depth those groups and people that socialize us, what sociologists call agents of socialization. In Chapter 3, we outline one of the key processes involved in socialization—the development of the self. Through this discussion it should be clear that who we are is fundamentally a function of our social world and the people around us.

The next few chapters examine important outcomes of socialization. In Chapter 4 we examine the concept of culture and explore how individuals are socialized within particular cultures. Our discussion of cultural variations in socialization practices reinforces the idea that socialization is a distinctly social process. Chapter 5 focuses on gender socialization, while Chapter 6 examines race and social class socialization. We show how each of these is a social construct, even though differences may appear to emerge from biological factors.

In Chapter 7 we turn our attention to adult socialization. Here we are reminded that socialization is a process and is never actually "completed." Throughout our lives we are confronted with new situations and adopt new roles and positions, and all of these require relearning how to be a part of a group. We follow this with a discussion in Chapter 8 of socialization "failures"—or at least what appears to be failures—those individuals who do not conform to the group norms. As you will see, these individuals push the boundaries of what is acceptable in a society and at times, help propel positive social change.

In the last chapter, Chapter 9, we provide a brief overview of socialization— what it is, how it occurs, and what it means for understanding ourselves and the world in which we live. We are reminded that socialization is vitally necessary for all human societies. Without it, our understanding of what it means to be human would take on a whole different meaning.

CHAPTER 1

BECOMING HUMAN

INTRODUCTION

What does it mean to be human?

This question has fascinated philosophers and great thinkers for hundreds of years, but it is also a question of significant interest to sociologists. From a sociological perspective, to be human is to be *socialized*. **Socialization** is the process by which individuals learn to be functioning members of society. To be "socialized," in other words, suggests that one understands the rules, customs, language, and symbols that characterize a particular culture and can draw upon these appropriately in social interaction.

Sociologists' particular take on the age-old question *What does it mean to be human?* leads us to additional questions. For example, how do we become human, or members of society? What does it mean to be part of such a culture? Is it possible not to be "human" or properly socialized? Answers to these questions point to one of the key subject areas of sociology: **socialization**.

In this chapter, we review the key concepts related to socialization and the assumptions sociologists make about the process. As you read further into the volume, you will see how these concepts and assumptions play out in a variety of ways.

THE IMPORTANCE OF SOCIALIZATION

Society could not function if individuals were not properly socialized. Imagine, for example, a society where people had no common language with which to communicate, lacking either the words or the ability to understand those words. Then imagine those same individuals not understanding what people in critical positions or roles do—for instance, what a friend or police officer was or did. Moreover, these individuals would not know how to dress, cross the street, sit, eat with utensils, or any of the thousands of things we take for granted and assume are inherent to human beings. Because such knowledge is deeply ingrained in most people (at least adults), it appears that people just *naturally* acquire such knowledge with no effort.

When socialization is successful, in fact, it appears to be "seamless" and unremarkable. But socialization does not happen automatically or by default. All individuals go through a process of socialization, and it takes a concerted effort by other members of society to ensure that new members learn what it means to be human within a particular social context. Such learning is critical to all individuals but also to society at large. If there were a serious breakdown in socialization, society as we know it would cease to exist.

WHAT IS LEARNED IN THE SOCIALIZATION PROCESS?

Anything that involves *social* learning—that is, related in any way to social relationships and interactions—involves socialization. The most basic bodily functions (breathing, elimination) are biologically driven (e.g., you don't have to learn how to breathe), but even these functions involve aspects of socialization. Have you ever tried to calm or control your breathing because you didn't want others to see how nervous you were? Have you ever fretted over finding a bathroom when you really needed one? Or closed the bathroom door before attending to the business of eliminating waste? Although both eliminating wastes and breathing are biological functions, socialization ensures that we also learn the appropriate ways to perform these acts.

Continuing with the bathroom example, we must learn first to *use* a toilet. Then we learn how much privacy is expected and how much to give others. At some point, we also learn how much and in what contexts discussion of one's elimination processes is appropriate (e.g., it may be appropriate to discuss such matters in a doctor's office but not at the dinner table). All of these practices, however, are culturally specific. In rural China, for example, there are no "bathrooms" per se, but public troughs where people eliminate wastes; many cultures have "squat toilets" rather than flush toilets; in many countries throughout the world, toilet paper is not used at all or cannot be flushed down the toilet. Even in the United States, there are major variations in bathroom behavior—in public spaces, men use urinals, women use toilets, and men's public bathrooms are considerably more "public" than women's. In other words, even the most basic human function is culturally specific, and the rules surrounding this function must be learned. Such learning occurs through the socialization process.

All social situations are governed by social norms, and learning how to behave in these situations is part of the socialization experience. Even actions that we don't normally think are social (such as being sick) are strongly governed by norms. Sociologist Talcott Parsons emphasized this point in his book *The Social System*. Parsons argued that even though illness involves physical pathology, there is a "sick role" that people are expected to play when they are ill. When people are sick, for example, they are excused from normal obligations and responsibilities and others are expected to care for them. People who are sick are also expected to want to feel better and to seek help as needed. Some people, of course, do not follow the rules. They violate social norms when they profess to be sick when they aren't, or they come to work while still sick and thus prolong their illness. Breaking the rules from the other side of illness are caregivers who do not provide appropriate assistance. If you have ever been in either of these situations or even in the presence of someone who is sick, you know how annoying it can be when someone breaks the norms of the sick role by coughing on everyone in the office or fakes being sick to get attention. If there were no norms surrounding being sick, your annoyance would not be understood; in fact, you would have no idea what we are describing here. The very fact that you do understand is evidence of socialization.

Take a moment to consider all the ways in which you are connected to others and the social world. You have friends, family, a job, school, leisure time; you belong to organizations or groups; you eat, sleep, and so on. Each of these activities involves socialization. Socialization is required to understand what it means to be a girl or boy, student, truck driver, fraternity member, religious or spiritual person, friend or enemy. Learning how to express emotions and to read others' emotional displays accurately, a process sociologist Steven Gordon calls **sentiment socialization**, is also part of socialization. So is learning how to transition successfully through life—how to be a child, an adolescent, a parent, a spouse, an old person—even how to approach death.

SOCIALIZATION THROUGHOUT LIFE

Socialization begins the moment a child is born. At birth, the child is assigned a sex, and from that point gender socialization begins in earnest. The parents usually provide some type of physical marker to communicate to everyone that their child is a boy or girl (e.g., an earring or bow for the girl; a blue outfit for the boy) because you can't really distinguish between most girl babies and boy babies unless they are undressed. Some of this may stem from simple enjoyment in dressing up the child, but much of it comes from a desire to communicate to the world the baby's gender so that others will know how to treat the child.

In cultures that emphasize independence, families are unlikely to share a family bed or have co-sleeping arrangements. Although the family bed is gaining greater popularity in the United States, this sleeping arrangement is far more common in other countries. *(Shutterstock)*

Studies show that parents and strangers alike treat boys and girls differently, even though the children's behavior or appearance are similar.

Gender is one important aspect of early socialization but there are many other things a child is taught early in life. Each child, for example, learns how and where to sleep (crib, cot, next to parents or alone), what and how to eat (from a bottle, a breast; whether and what types of animals are considered appropriate food), who responds to cries and who doesn't, and so on. All this learning is critical not only to the child's physical survival but also as a means of acquiring deep understanding of the values and expectations of the culture in which the child will have to interact. In the United States, for example, *independence* is a highly valued trait, probably one reason babies and children are expected to sleep alone. In collectivist cultures that value cooperation and interdependence, babies would most likely sleep in a "family bed."

As a child ages, new social experiences form part of the socialization process. In fact, socialization is never complete. Adults also go through socialization (or *re*socialization) as new roles and cultural experiences occur. Recall when you first entered high school or a new school. You probably felt lost, apprehensive, and unsure of yourself. Some of the questions you may have asked yourself (or others) show how much you had to figure out: What are the rules? Who do I sit with at lunch? Who are the people or groups I need to know (perhaps to hang around with, perhaps to avoid)? Which classes are hard? Which teachers are best? What's the school song? What's the dress code? Once you became socialized, you began to feel part of the school environment.

Some sociologists believe that socialization does not end until you die, assuming you do not die a social isolate (very few do). Most people entering old age must learn new identities, for example, how to be a "retiree" or "grandmother" or "senior citizen." They must also learn to give up previous identities such as executive or wife/husband when the spouse dies. Moving into a nursing home or assisted living facility also requires new learning and socialization. Often, it also requires facing death.

Victor Marshall's research on retirement home residents illustrates how norms govern the dying process. The residents at Glen Brae, where he conducted his research, are aware that death is impending even though the facility's motto is that it "is a place to come to and live; not to die." As Marshall explains, "People do die at Glen Brae, and they go there knowing they will die there." His

Aging and dying involve socialization. Among the many changes to which the elderly must adapt, new living arrangements may constrain social interactions and introduce new social challenges. Here, Rear Admiral James A. Symonds visits a resident of a nursing home care center. *(Wikipedia)*

research, moreover, showed that residents had ideas about how they wanted to die. For example, one resident said "I hope to live comfortably and not be too much of a care to my children. And to die 'gracefully.' I aim to die without yelling, 'Hey, I'm going.'" As Marshall notes, "Living in a community of the dying, these people 'know' what is a good and what is a bad style of dying." In other words, there are personal and social expectations associated with dying. These expectations are learned from watching others and thinking about one's own imminent death. Interestingly, residents were not afraid of death, but they were afraid of dying, a distinction that underscores the fact that dying is a social process, governed by norms and expectations, and those engaged in that process are socialized into the "dying role."

SOCIALIZATION AS PROCESS

When people say someone is socialized, they often have in mind the "end product." That is, they are thinking of a person who is a functioning member of society—someone who understands the rules, customs, and expectations of that culture. Indeed, even much scholarly attention to socialization focuses on the *outcome* of socialization. But this approach misses out on a very interesting question—just how did this person become socialized? It also assumes that there *is* an end product.

Many sociologists, including the authors of this volume, would argue that socialization is never finished. In effect, there really isn't an "end product" or final outcome of socialization. Rather, socialization is an ongoing **process** that lasts throughout one's life. Some individuals have been at it longer than others, but no one can be said to be completely socialized. An individual can become more proficient at a task or in a role, and even teach it to others, but as people and cultures change, so too can the expectations associated with that role or task. Society is too vast and social life too fluid for anyone to ever have a complete grasp of the expectations and norms governing social life.

Therefore, socialization is about "becoming" and "doing" rather than "being." It is a process, not an outcome or end-product. Consider something most people think is an end product of socialization—one's gender. Most people just *know* how to be a woman or man, it doesn't take a lot of conscious thought. But how is a man socialized to believe that boys don't cry supposed to act when attending the funeral of his best friend? How is a woman who is raised to believe girls should be nice and nonaggressive supposed to act when she is playing college basketball? The point is that these (and similar) situations call for new ways of being masculine or feminine. They require new skills and new views on how masculine and feminine are "done"—at least in certain social contexts. Even gender socialization—something that many think is accomplished in early childhood—continues throughout one's lifetime and requires relearning as circumstances change.

SOCIALIZATION AS AN ACTIVE PROCESS

Early conceptualizations of socialization presented it as a one-way process, what can be thought of as the **deterministic model of socialization**. That is, a child was thought to be a "blank slate" or "tabula rasa." According to this theory, adults filled children's minds with cultural knowledge, and children soaked up such knowledge like passive little sponges. Adults, peers, media and others, could thus imprint on children the norms, values, and ideals of society. In her book, *Gender Play*, Barrie Thorne summarizes this model as follows: "Adults are said to socialize children, teachers socialize students, the more powerful socialize, and the less powerful get socialized."

Thorne and other sociologists now reject this deterministic model of socialization, arguing that children actually play very active roles in the socialization process. They do not simply absorb everything. Rather, they exercise some degree of **agency**, or control, over the process. William Corsaro explores this concept in his book *The Sociology of Childhood*. Corsaro argues for a **constructivist model of socialization** (so called because children help to construct the process), a model that sees the child as an eager and active participant in his or her own learning. Sociologists such as Corsaro actually prefer a different term than "socialization," which he claims is too individualistic and future-oriented. He notes: "One hears the term and the idea of training and preparing the individual child for the future keeps coming right back to mind." Corsaro prefers the term **interpretative reproduction**, which captures children's creative and innovative involvement in society; Thorne uses the metaphor of *play* to illuminate children's active engagement in social life. Although we use the term "socialization" in this volume, we agree with the constructivist model and attempt to highlight children's and adults' agency in all aspects of social life.

At a basic level, children may exercise agency by negotiating "deals" with parents or others to alter rules adults try to impose on them. For example, the teenage girl whose parents want her to be "girly" may convince her parents to let her play lacrosse; she in turn, may take extra care to act feminine in other ways to appease her parents. Children and adolescents who reject their religious or political upbringing are also exercising agency. Understanding socialization as involving agency can help explain why kids sometimes act so different from the way they've been raised.

A further example of what is meant by agency can clarify what is implied about the active role individuals play in the socialization process and the contrast between the deterministic and constructivist models. From a deterministic perspective, one would assume that media images that present beautiful models with "perfect" bodies have a negative impact on young women because these individuals passively absorb the messages about how women's bodies should look. But sociologist Melissa Milkie studied a group of adolescent girls

Magazine cover. Minority women claim to not identify with images in magazines as much as white women do, and therefore may be better able to resist messages that emphasize beauty and thinness. *(Joel Saget/AFP/Getty Images)*

as they interacted with media images. *Interact* is a key word here. Milkie found that girls did not passively absorb images they saw in magazines. Rather they were often critical of the images, as this quotation from one girl shows:

. . . these magazines are trying to tell you "Do this and do that." Sometimes they have . . . swimsuits and stuff, and what you can do if you have a problem body . . . And these girls that they are showing don't have that problem. I mean you can tell they don't, and that makes me mad. . . . They say if you got a stick figure, wear a one-piece and . . . colorful and I'm looking at the girl and she doesn't have a stick figure.

Milkie found that minority girls were especially critical of magazine images because they did not identify with the white models.

This and similar examples clearly illustrate that individuals are not passive participants in the socialization process. They are active agents, who can resist, question, or renegotiate the messages they receive from the world around them. Another simple example illustrates how this works:

Agency can be seen in the ways women negotiate beauty messages. Here, a young woman seeks to redefine feminine beauty as stronger and bolder than traditional messages suggest. *(Shutterstock)*

Adolescent girls receive strong messages about the importance of beauty and looking attractive to men. Girls may resist these messages by deliberating dressing down; they may question these messages, as the girls in Milkie's study did when they wondered whether the models were real; or they can renegotiate by redefining what is "beautiful."

THE ROLE OF LANGUAGE IN SOCIALIZATION

By now you know that to become a fully functional member of society, certain cognitive, linguistic, and biological skills must be acquired and mastered; but socialization is fundamentally a *social* process. Meanings and understandings about the self and society, and everything in between, arise through social interactions. The primary mechanism that drives this process is **language**. Through language—a complex set of shared and commonly understood verbal and nonverbal sounds and gestures that express ideas and feelings—we are able to communicate with one another about the most mundane and profound aspects of social life and ourselves. Language serves as a bridge between the individual and a larger group or culture. If you speak the language of the group or culture, you can "belong."

Through the process of acquiring language, a child begins to label objects in her world. "Objects" refer to everything—grass, lettuce, police officer, chair, friend, mom, one's body, one's self. With these labels come shared understandings about the significance and purpose of these objects, and how they connect and interact with other objects. For instance, a child gradually learns that the person who tucks him in at night (among many other things) is "Daddy." But he will also learn that there are many "daddies" out there, so his becomes "My Dad," setting this particular man apart from others. In the process, the child learns more and more about what fathers do and how they interact with their children, and he also learns that there's a big difference between "my dad" and other "dads." His father is someone he can depend upon to help him with

Common Human Language?

You may have heard people say that laughter (or love) is the common human language. There is some truth in this. If you hope to negotiate a legal contract, or settle a fight between friends or nations, or figure out whether you and your spouse will cook in or go out to eat tonight, having a shared *verbal* language is necessary. But in matters of basic survival, you need to know if someone is friend or foe, angry or happy. This type of information is communicated primarily through *nonverbal* language. Studies show that persons throughout the world can accurately "read" basic human emotions when shown photographs.

Interestingly, even these basic expressions of emotion can be learned and manipulated. Sociologists are interested in **emotion work**—the efforts we make to bring our emotions in line with cultural expectations. For instance, a waitress is expected to be cordial and pleasant, even when she is deeply irritated and angry at a customer. She learns, through socialization, how to suppress her anger and manipulate her facial expressions to conceal her real feelings. It is not always easy to differentiate between facial expressions that are sincere or those that are deliberately arranged to conceal something or serve another specific purpose.

(opposite page: **Test yourself here to see how well you can read human emotions through nonverbal cues.** *(Shutterstock/Wikipedia)*

his homework, play games with him, and listen to his endless stories about his day at school. The child also begins to understand that he can't expect other dads to do that. It is in this way that language is a key to becoming socialized because understanding language means understanding shared meanings, and it is through shared meanings that children come to understand the expectations and rules of society.

ANTICIPATORY SOCIALIZATION

One important aspect of socialization is what sociologist Robert Merton called **anticipatory socialization.** This process occurs when individuals expect to move into different roles or jobs, and begin acquiring the skills, knowledge, and attitudes appropriate to the new role. For example, soldiers preparing to return to civilian life begin to anticipate that transition and make changes and adopt attitudes of the group they expect to rejoin.

Anticipatory socialization is commonplace because people are continuously transitioning into new situations and roles. You did when you entered school for the first time, when you moved from elementary school to junior high, then into high school or college. If you work or date or got married, you made significant transitions toward adulthood. In each of these instances, you most likely engaged in anticipatory socialization by starting to acquire some of the "markers" associated with the new identity (e.g., clothes, language, attitudes) and also by letting go of the old markers (e.g., throwing out childhood toys or pictures of old girlfriends). An interesting example of this comes from Randi Wærdahl's study of Norwegian youth on the verge of leaving elementary school and going to junior high school. The title of Wærdahl's article—"Maybe I'll need a pair of Levi's before junior high?"—came from an interview with a young girl who was anticipating what it meant to transition from childhood to young adulthood. In Norway, Levi jeans are prized possessions and status symbols, far too expensive and unnecessary for most parents to buy for their preadolescents. The youth in Wærdahl's study would consciously forego the symbols of childhood (including childish fashions and activities) and adopt those of the older group to which they aspired to belong, such as jeans.

Consider another form of anticipatory socialization: children's "make-believe." This favorite children's game allows them to role-play superheroes, mommies, doctors, and so on. In essence, as children are playing and engaging in these various activities, they are actually learning how to be competent providers, workers, and parents. In other words, when a child actually steps into the role of "spouse" or "nurse," that child has practiced the role and has to some degree incorporated into his or her identity the qualities associated with these positions and roles.

Anticipatory socialization does not simply happen during playtime or during major transitions. In many ways, we are practicing future roles and the many dimensions of these roles by performing very common activities. For instance, consider how the experience of going to summer camp could help prepare you for going off to college. You must venture out into the big world, make new friends, sleep in a strange place without your mom or dad, and trust other people to teach you what you need to know. Incidentally, anticipatory socialization occurs at all ages. When your parent dropped you off at summer camp or kindergarten for the first time, he or she was also learning how to manage the emotions and grant you greater independence which came or will come in handy when it is time to drop you off at college or walk you down the aisle.

Dating is a classic example of anticipatory socialization for marriage. Through dating, individuals can practice all the things that will be needed to form and maintain a successful partnership. You learn how to negotiate and compromise with another person, how to maintain your individuality but also be coupled, you experiment with sexual intimacy, you meet your partner's parents and family, you learn how to read another person's moods and what his or her "buttons" are. It is interesting to note that as traditional dating has declined

By "playing house" children can practice certain skills that may later be called into practice when they grow up to be parents and spouses. *(Heinrich Schönhauser. Wikipedia)*

and couples are more likely to interact with groups or simply hook up, many individuals question whether they are really ready for marriage.

CULTURAL VARIATIONS IN SOCIALIZATION

Every society or culture has its own ways of doing things. If you've ever traveled outside of your country, you can readily recall examples of how cultural practices vary. Even English-speaking countries have different words for objects. For example, a "salad" in England is what you put on a sandwich, not something served in a separate dish. Such cultural practices are always rooted in the historical and social reality. The classic film *Pulp Fiction* illustrates this point nicely: Vincent Vega (played by John Travolta) asks his partner, Jules Winnfield (played by Samuel L. Jackson), if he knows what a *Quarter Pounder with Cheese* is called in Paris? Jules assumes they call it the same thing so Vincent explains: "No, man, they got the metric system, they don't know what . . . a Quarter Pounder is."

It is important to remember that it's not just words that vary from country to country. Expectations surrounding social roles also differ across cultures. In some cultures or groups, it is commonplace, even expected, that wives will work outside the home for pay. In other countries, women may work hard but not for pay. Thus, what it means to be a "wife" will vary and socialization into the "wife" role is specific to a particular cultural context. When women who are raised with one set of expectations move into a different cultural context, confusion and conflict can occur. Consider, for example, the challenge facing an American military wife who moves her family to a Muslim country, where women's ability to travel alone is quite different from that of women in the United States.

SOCIAL STRUCTURE AND SOCIALIZATION

We have emphasized the creative, active role that children play in the socialization process but that is not the whole story. While it is true that children (and adults) can exercise agency, they are also constrained by **social structure**, which refers to all the ways in which society guides individuals' actions to produce patterned behaviors and interactions. Neither children nor adults are free to act in any way they please. They are constrained or limited by society, sometimes through **social control** (e.g., through laws and norms), as well as by limitations on what is even possible. For example, when concerts are planned and designed, there are performers on stage and an audience seated or standing somewhere besides the stage and the performer–fan relationship becomes defined as "them–us." Another example illustrating the establishment of such limits can be seen in the way teaching and learning occurs in most universities and colleges. An instructor may wish to do away with grading because he believes it encourages students to focus on the wrong things and interferes with learning. The plan cannot be implemented, however, because the institution insists that teachers give grades.

Social control can have a significant effect on behavior and can even stifle agency. The couple madly in love and desperately wanting to marry is likely to be dissuaded by social control if one or both fear being disowned by an angry parent or if one or both families are expected to react violently. But social control does not always take the form of "others." It can also stem from an internalized sense of fear. Most women, for example, would welcome the freedom of dressing however they please and walking alone at night, but few do. Simply the fear of what might happen and what people would think if something did happen ("How could you be so stupid?" or "Well, what did you expect?") is enough to constrain most women's behavior.

Thus, despite individual agency and ability, our social reality is almost constantly constrained and affected by social norms and institutions. Few escape this fate; those who cannot or will not conform to the limits set by those norms and institutions often pay a price for doing so.

CAN INDIVIDUALS NOT BE SOCIALIZED?
Individuals may have a certain amount of agency or ability to resist socialization messages, but because we operate within a larger social structure, it is virtually impossible to avoid being socialized or learning what others expect of you. We may hear people say that someone has not been properly socialized or even that someone is "unsocialized." But what might appear as incomplete or faulty socialization may in fact be the opposite. For example, a "deviant" individual may appear to have little regard for social norms—wearing strange clothes, cursing aloud in public, or engaging in any number of seemingly inappropriate or criminal actions. But deviant cultures, which have been studied extensively by sociologists, are in fact governed by strong social norms. They simply differ from those of the mainstream culture. Indeed, socialization within a deviant culture may be highly successful—so much so that it has led the individual to deviate from mainstream culture and adopt a different set of values, in this case values that condone or even reward wearing clothes that the dominant cultures deems strange and engaging in behavior that the dominant culture deems inappropriate, offensive, or even criminal.

In certain cases, individuals who are perceived to be "not socialized" are also deemed unable to function in human society and are "removed" from that society. Some are confined to institutions (such as prisons), perhaps even executed. In such cases, we might say that socialization has been unsuccessful because if the purpose of socialization is to produce functioning members of society, socialization has failed. But in the case of criminals, sociologists would argue that no one operates solely in an individualistic world—not even criminals—and that all individuals are influenced (and socialized) by larger norms.

It is for this reason that you are more likely to find violent criminals in societies that value and tolerate violence.

Other "unsocialized" individuals may have mental or physical conditions that limit or prohibit communication with others. And (as we have briefly discussed earlier in this volume) communication is the key to socialization. If communication cannot or does not occur, socialization cannot and does not occur. An extreme example comes from what we know about **feral children**, a term used to designate children who have been raised in social isolation, cut off from almost all human interaction. One of the most famous cases is a child known as "Genie." Genie came to the attention of authorities in California after spending 13 years locked away, with virtually no human contact. Although the facts of this sad case are not entirely known, it appears that no one spoke to her during those 13 years and that her captor(s) interacted with her only in the most primitive and abusive ways (e.g., strapping her to a potty chair during the daytime or beating her whenever she vocalized). When she was discovered, Genie could speak no more than 20 words; she mostly spat and clawed when around people. She did not walk upright. Although Genie later acquired some language skills, she was never able to have anything resembling a normal life. She moved from one foster home to another and is currently living in an adult foster home in California.

Studies of feral children reveal the importance of communication and human interaction as a prerequisite for socialization. Without such contact, it is impossible for a child (or adult) to learn the norms, values, and language of a group or society, or even have a sense of oneself. From a sociological perspective, such an individual will never be fully human.

KEY PRINCIPLES

In this chapter we have reviewed the basic principles of socialization. As you read through this volume, you will see how these key principles operate with respect to socialization in such things as gender, race, class, culture, and identity. There are a few main points to keep in mind:

- Socialization is the process by which individuals learn to be functioning members of society.
- The key to becoming a member of any group (and to successful socialization) is language. Language involves understanding common meanings of gestures and sounds. Without shared language, it is not possible to communicate expected cultural practices and values.
- All societies socialize their members; this is essential if a society is to function.

- Because cultures differ from one another, the content of socialization varies across groups and societies.
- Socialization is a life-long process; it does not end in childhood and is never "complete."
- Anticipatory socialization occurs as individuals acquire (or expect to acquire) new roles; it is a way of preparing themselves for these new roles by "practicing" the skills, language, and behaviors associated with them.
- Persons who are being socialized play an active role in this learning process.
- Socialization is reciprocal. Although one individual or group may be targeted for social learning, those who are designated as "teachers" are also being socialized.
- Although individuals have agency (the ability to resist or reject messages they receive), they exist within a larger social structure that constrains and limits individual choices and behavior.
- As long as individuals interact with others, socialization occurs. It is possible for the socialization process to break down, however, if individuals are kept isolated from others.

Further Reading

Corsaro, William. *The Sociology of Childhood*. Thousand Oaks, Calif.: Pine Forge Press, 1997.

Gubrium, Jaber F. *Living and Dying at Murray Manor*. Charlottesville: University Press of Virginia, 1997.

Marshall, Victor W. "Socialization for impending death in a retirement village." *American Journal of Sociology* 80 (1975): 1124–1144.

Milkie, Melissa A. "Social comparisons, reflected appraisals, and mass media: The impact of pervasive beauty images on black and white girls' self-concepts." *Social Psychology Quarterly* 62 (1999): 190–210.

NOVA: Secret of the Wild Child. Date aired: March 4, 1997. http://www.pbs.org/

CHAPTER 2

WHO AND WHAT SOCIALIZES US

As you learned in Chapter 1, socialization is not a one-way process, something handed down from adults to children in a standard and predictable fashion. It is, instead, a process that involves reciprocal learning. Children are not "blank slates" upon which others write the rules of society; while they are learning about society and being socialized, they are also teaching (or helping to socialize) adults and other children in the process.

At the same time, there is no question that adults and social institutions exert considerable influence on children. Some adults are explicitly assigned the "job" of socializing children, as is the case of parents, teachers, and youth leaders. Adults also play key roles within social institutions (e.g., schools and families) that structure children's lives. Within these institutions and groups, adults are given authority to control and shape children's values and actions within specific settings. That is, adults have the culturally given right to control children's actions. In this context, they become and function as **agents of socialization**.

AGENTS OF SOCIALIZATION

Agents of socialization are not always individuals; they are also important groups or institutions that are considered to be highly influential in teaching people about culture and norms and often have the explicit job of socializing others. Thus, agents of socialization are those persons or institutions that exert tremendous pressure on others to act in certain ways and therefore, play a major role in socialization. Some of the most powerful agents of socialization are parents, peers and siblings, media, teachers (including coaches and youth leaders), and religious leaders. Obviously not everyone has the same influences operating in their lives, and for some people, certain people or groups will be more influential than others. But these agents of socialization are integral to society and as a result, virtually everyone's lives are shaped by these individuals to some degree.

The relative importance of any particular agent of socialization will vary by an individual's circumstances and age. For instance, in very early childhood, parents or guardians exert the greatest influence on children, teaching them everything from how to eat with proper utensils to playing cooperatively with friends. For children whose parents, for whatever reason, are not able or willing to perform this role, other individuals (e.g., grandparents, older siblings, foster care parents) will step in to provide this early and intense socialization.

As children get older, however, they come into greater contact with other people and situations that shape their lives. It may help to think about this broadening as a series of concentric circles. In the middle, the center, is the child. The child's first major contact and influence are the parents or guardians. Gradually, the child comes in contact with other adults such as daycare providers or grandparents who teach different skills, values, and cultural knowledge. Later, the child is likely to form friendships, and this means contact with peers as well as peers' parents and other family members. Gradually, the number of interactions grows, and the child is exposed to media, teachers, coaches, religious leaders, and other adults and children. All of these individuals and institutions have the potential of serving as powerful agents of socialization. Here we examine a few of the most important influences in greater detail.

Parents

The first and arguably the most important agents of socialization are parents (or individuals who assume parental roles) because they provide the first real link to others and to the outside world. It is from parents that children learn that police officers should be trusted (or not), that it's important to be politically engaged (or not), that women need to learn to rely upon themselves and not men (or not), and literally millions of other pieces of discreet cultural knowledge that make up their understanding of the world. Moreover, much of what children learn from parents is so deeply ingrained that they cannot consciously remember a time when they did not know these things.

Evidence of parental influence over children's ways of thinking and behaving can be seen in studies of political affiliations. It is in fact possible to predict a person's political leanings and values with a high degree of accuracy if you know just one thing—the parents' political affiliation. Children's religious values and behaviors are also likely to resemble those of their parents.

Interestingly, in immigrant families, where parents are less knowledgeable than children about U.S. culture and politics, socialization is a much more bidirectional or a "bottom-up" process. Political scientists Janelle Wong and Vivian Tseng found that children of immigrants are likely to have more experience and knowledge about U.S. politics than their parents, so in these families political socialization "trickles-up" from children to parents. Parents may be teaching their children about their native country's political landscape, but children teach parents about U.S. politics.

Because in most families, women tend to be the primary caretakers of children (which in itself teaches children about women's and men's expected roles), mothers or other primary female guardians often play a particularly powerful role in shaping children's beliefs and behaviors. But in many families in the United States and in Western societies in general, fathers have begun to play an increasingly important role in children's lives. Data from the U.S. Bureau of Census shows that of the 11.3 million preschoolers whose mothers work outside the home, 25 percent are cared for by their fathers while their mothers are

Even though mothers continue to assume primary responsibility for children, the number of stay-at-home fathers and single-parent households headed by men have increased significantly in recent years. *(Wikipedia)*

working. There are approximately 1.8 million single-parent households headed by fathers and about 140,000 married men who are stay-at-home dads. These numbers have been increasing in recent decades.

Even in families where women are still primary caretakers, fathers are powerful agents of socialization. Studies show that fathers are important to children's development because their active participation in childrearing means greater parental involvement. This greater involvement seems to be related to higher intellectual development in children, probably as a result of the multiple benefits derived from attention and knowledge coming from two individuals rather than one. Moreover, fathers often have a different type of relationship with children than mothers do, and fathers often teach children skills and values that are distinct from those the children learn from their mothers. In her book *Do Men Mother?* sociologist Andrea Doucet suggests that fathers specialize in fun and physical play; they promote risk-taking and independence and thus offer something unique to children.

Because U.S. culture has increasingly shifted from the "traditional" mother-father-children family to a variety of nontraditional family forms, you might well be wondering what happens in families that do not have two parents or families that have two same-sex parents. How does the socializing of children occur in such family units? Is it deficient or lacking in any significant way? There are no simple answers to these questions. Most sociologists would argue that there is nothing innately gendered about good parenting. In other words, fathers can be just as nurturing as women and when circumstances dictate, a man can be as good (or bad) a parent as a woman. Mothers can (and often do) teach children a wide range of tasks and skills and social understandings that we might associate with being masculine. But children raised in single-parent households are more likely to be disadvantaged educationally and economically than those raised by two parents, perhaps because single parents have less time to spend with children and are much more likely to be financially strapped than their two-parent-family counterparts.

On the other hand, studies of children raised in same-sex households find that children raised by two mothers or two fathers are not disadvantaged. Sociologists Timothy Biblarz and Judith Stacey conducted an extensive review of literature on whether children raised by two men or two women differ significantly from those raised by heterosexual couples on a wide range of outcomes related to children's well-being. They found that children raised with a father and mother are no more likely than those raised in same-sex households, especially by two women, to be emotionally, socially, or cognitively advantaged. In fact, the researchers conclude that being raised by two women led to greater parental investment and better relationships between parents and children, perhaps because women (straight or lesbian) tend to spend more time than men with children. They note:

. . . one could argue that two women parent better on average than a woman and a man, or at least than a woman and man with a traditional division of family labor. Lesbian co-parents seem to outperform comparable married heterosexual, biological parents on several measures, even while being denied the substantial privileges of marriage. This seems to be attributable partly to selection effects and partly to women on average exceeding men in parenting investment and skills.

Regardless of family form, parents—whether they be male or female, single or coupled, straight or gay/lesbian—are primary agents of socialization. But an important point here is that all 21st-century parents face a particularly difficult job of socialization. As you probably know, in the majority of two-parent families, both parents work long hours outside the home; in one-parent families, this is even more necessary as one income is more difficult to stretch from paycheck to paycheck. In addition, there has been increased pressure in recent decades on parents to provide everything for their children, with no help from outside the family circle. This phenomenon of increased expectations on parents (especially mothers) to provide for all of their children's needs has been labeled **intensive mothering** by Sharon Hays. Sociologist Jennifer Glass elaborates on this point: "Parents are now responsible for an exhausting number of functions in their children's lives." A sampling of what Glass says parents are now expected to do for their children follows:

- Mothers should breastfeed for at least a year, despite the failure of employers to accommodate breastfeeding in any reasonable way . . .
- Parents are supposed to provide healthy, well-balanced meals and opportunities for exercise, and protect their children from the dangers of unsafe water, food, or exposure to the sun . . .
- Parents must sit with their children when they watch TV or go to movies, to protect them from exposure to excessive media violence or sexually explicit content, and monitor their internet use to avoid exposure to adult Web sites or pedophiles in chat rooms . . .
- Parents are to teach their children moral values and prosocial behavior, and are held accountable when children succumb to the myriad temptations to engage in inappropriate or antisocial behavior . . .
- When children are older, parents must get to know their friends and their friends' parents and watch for precocious sexual activity, bulimia in their daughters, and aggression in their sons . . .

Glass's point here is not to remind us of how difficult the job of parenting is but to emphasize that demands on parents are greater today than in earlier historical periods and harder in part because demands on workers have also escalated. Thus, parental socialization has become more challenging and bordering on impossible. Although some parents can afford outside help, many cannot, and children are left to navigate the complexities of childhood and adolescence with less parental guidance, or with the help of friends and other family.

If all parents have a challenging job of socializing children, imagine how challenging this is for those who parent "outside the norm." Same-sex parents, parents of interracial or minority children, parents of disabled children, and so on, have even greater challenges. For example, in her book *Unequal Childhoods,* Annette Lareau noted how one black middle-class family had to attend to the issues of race in a way that white middle-class parents rarely have to think about:

> We have been very careful not to put him in situations where he is the only Black child. We've been very careful about that. Not only is that not fair, but we've also been careful to make sure he mixed with a group . . . let's say of white kids whose parents . . . uh . . . are cultured. You know. They've been introduced to many different types of people and can accept that there are differences in people in a positive manner.

Parents of color must teach their children to survive in two cultures: the dominant "white" culture and the non-white culture with which they are associated. This is especially challenging when one parent was raised in one culture but must prepare his or her child to live in another. How do you teach someone what you yourself may only understand on an intellectual basis? It is for this reason, in fact, that the National Association of Black Social Workers opposes transracial adoption (e.g., two white parents adopting a black child), claiming that the parents of a child of a different race, no matter how hard they may try, may find it nearly impossible to teach that child about racism and be racial role models for that child.

Of course, many biracial families have parents of different races and can thus provide important racial socialization for children. But, as we've previously noted, it is the mothers that are most likely to assume primary childrearing responsibilities in families. If the mothers are white, they may find racial socialization a challenging prospect. One of the most poignant accounts of biracial parenting can be found in Maureen Reddy's *Crossing the Color Line.* Reddy describes the moment she realized that her dark-skinned son (he is of African American and Irish American descent), playing hide-and-seek in the bushes outside her house, could be mistaken for criminal rather than being seen simply as a child playing a friendly game. She also describes the challenge of teaching her son about biracialism:

Sean first asserted his biracialism during a dinner table discussion of a meeting I planned to attend with other parents of black children. "But Mom," he interjected, "you don't have black children. Why are you going?"

Thinking this was a joke, I laughed and said, "So, what are you, then, chopped liver?"

"No," he answered very seriously, "but I'm not black either. I'm black and white."

A mundane exchange of information . . . had turned into a parenting crisis. Was Sean denying his blackness? Would he prefer to be white?. . . We'd been surrounding him with countless images of black achievement and black pride from infancy . . . what had gone wrong? I . . . was suffused with guilt and shame, perceiving Sean's assertion as an indictment of my mothering . . .

All parents, regardless of their circumstances, have the important job of socializing their children to be fully functioning members of society. This involves teaching them how to navigate the sometimes harsh and even hostile reactions of others. Unquestionably, some parents have a more challenging task at hand than others. What makes this task especially difficult is that parents are just one socialization agent, and the messages parents provide may be contradicted by others as children move further into the world.

Siblings

If you have a brother or sister, you can probably remember a time when he or she helped you learn a new task or skill or opened your mind to a new way of solving a problem or conflict. Surprisingly little has been studied and written within the discipline of sociology about the importance of siblings in the socialization process. What we know about siblings as socializing agents is mostly anecdotal, but it is not hard to find these cases. Consider, for instance, basketball great Isiah Thomas. In Thomas's book *The Fundamentals: Eight Plays for Winning the Games of Business and Life* he attributes his success to his brother Larry, who taught him the fundamentals of basketball and trained him as a young child. Drew Brees, quarterback for the New Orleans Saints, talks about his close relationship with his brother Reid, and how they became inseparable after their parents divorced. Such stories remind us that our siblings can be particularly powerful agents of socialization, regardless of whether parents are present or not.

Teachers and Schools

Teachers are in a position to have a particularly profound effect on children's socialization. This is especially true for young children because school teachers often serve as quasi-parents. Given the amount of time children are in school, teachers have the potential to be especially powerful agents of socialization.

Teachers are believed to be powerful transmitters of knowledge about gender, race, and social class. Many times, they may not be aware of the messages they are delivering, but their words and actions (what they condone or punish, which child they call on in class and which child they ignore, and so on) convey powerful messages to children about their value in society and social expectations.

Ann Ferguson, in her fascinating book entitled *Bad Boys: Public Schools in the Making of Black Masculinity,* shares some of the subtle ways in which such messages are transmitted to youth. In the following poignant example, Ferguson recalls a teacher reprimanding two African American girls (in the presence of several boys) for being too rowdy in the hallway. Here's Ferguson's account:

> Miss Benton is yelling at the girls because they have been jumping in the hallway . . . This is what she says: "You're doing exactly what they want you to do. You're playing into their hands. . . . Next year they're going to be tracking you."
>
> One of the girls asks her rather sullenly who "they" is.
>
> Miss Benton is furious. "Society, that's who. You should be leading the class, not fooling around jumping around in the hallway. Someone has to give pride to the community. All the black men are on drugs, or in jail, or killing each other. Someone has to hold it together. And the women have to do it...."

On the one hand, this exchange could be seen as a teacher concerned about the girls' futures and as someone who is taking her job as a socializing agent seriously. On the other hand, think about what message(s) these girls (and the boys who witnessed the encounter) received. As Ferguson notes: "Tracks have already been laid down for sixth-grade girls toward a specifically feminized responsibility (and, what is more prevalent, blame) for the welfare of the community, while males are bound for jail as a consequence of their own socially and self-destructive acts."

One of the most important lessons Ferguson imparts is that when children exhibit identical behaviors, they are treated differently, depending upon their gender and race. First, teachers can decide whether to "notice" the behavior in the first place; if they do, they must then decide whether and what type of disciplinary action should be taken. Teachers notice young black males' behaviors more than those of girls or white boys, even if those behaviors are the same. Because of this, teachers contribute to the already prevalent message given to African American boys—they are troublemakers with limited prospects for the future.

Homeschooling

Given the importance of schools and teachers to children's socialization, it is interesting to consider whether children who are not exposed to schools and traditional teachers miss out on importance experiences and learning. The U.S. Census estimates that about 1.5 million children are homeschooled. There are many reasons why parents may choose to home school their children, but there are two common features: homeschooled children receive their education in less formal settings, and the primary "teacher" is usually a parent. Questions about the practice focus on the following themes: Without regular interaction with other children their ages, do homeschooled children miss out on important socialization experiences? Does homeschooling prevent or limit anticipatory socialization? And if so, will homeschooled children be poorly equipped to function in the "real world" (e.g., the workplace) as adults?

Sharon Bouma studied families who homeschooled and found that parents adopt strategies to provide their children with the social and educational opportunities they might miss by not being in a traditional classroom. She notes that homeschooled children have more time and opportunity to interact with society outside of school on a daily basis than children who attend traditional school. Moreover, homeschooled children typically spend time at public libraries and in community or volunteer activities, in organized activities (e.g., scouting, sports, writing circles), and with other homeschooling families or support groups, where they interact with adults and children of all ages. In addition, they are also often involved in the ordinary tasks involved in running a household (such as running errands, paying bills, and shopping). All of these experiences help homeschooled children develop important social skills. In the end, these children may acquire skills and knowledge about how to "think outside the box" because they must sometimes seek alternative routes to getting their socialization needs met. The sidebar on the subject of homeschooling illustrates this concept and is the personal account of Sharon Bouma's daughter.

Bouma notes that one thing all homeschooled children "miss out on" is working with assigned teachers and other students. In this sense, homeschooled children may be somewhat less prepared for the workplace, where one's choice of co-workers and boss is limited, and where dealing with difficult co-workers or unpleasant work demands are common. Most parents of homeschooled children, however, argue that adults have the option to negotiate or simply resign from work situations that are unworkable for them. Thus they do not see the need for their children to practice these skills (i.e., dealing with a variety of assigned teachers and with classmates), especially as their time is better spent on developing their own character and personalities.

If we also consider that educational institutions (like all social institutions) largely function to reproduce existing systems, including inequality, it could be argued that homeschooled children are not exposed to many potentially negative messages concerning gender, race, and social class that children in traditional schools receive from teachers. Of course, parents can be and often are the source of such messages, but homeschoolers can more easily counter them than

Homeschooling: A Personal Account

When I was 12 years old, I found myself feeling lonely. I had no problem making friends when I was younger, including play dates with other kids in homeschooling groups; but when I entered the middle school years, my friends were mostly from my dance, drama, choir, and book groups. These activities gave me experience in dealing with some of the tougher issues of socialization, including bullying, peer pressure, and teachers or group leaders who made unfair demands on their students. However, most of my extracurricular activities were in a city that was a 45-minute drive away from the town where I lived, so I usually only saw my friends once a week at practices. This made it hard for us to form strong bonds of friendship. I solved my need for closer friendships by becoming pen pals with several other girls my age. I found my first pen pals via listings in a homeschooling magazine. We shared names and networked, and within a couple of years I had more than 25 pen pals from all over the United States and the world. I discovered that it was easy to form close, lasting relationships with other girls my age who were also interested in writing letters. I still keep in touch with several of them, including my best friend, who was my first pen pal. (Elizabeth Holtrop, 2010).

children in schools can. For example, a homeschooled girl may be unaware of the stereotype that "girls are bad at math" until she finds herself one of just a few teenage girls competing in the Math Quiz Bowl. Because the stereotype is foreign to her, she is likely to resist this cultural message or consider it more critically than children who attend schools would.

The case of homeschoolers reveals other important points concerning socialization. First, socialization occurs even if traditional structures and processes are absent or modified. The traditional agents of socialization may differ, but others will take their place. Second, although socialization is designed primarily so that individuals can perform existing roles within society, people who have been homeschooled can modify and adapt socialization experiences to align more closely with personal values and circumstances.

Other Adults as Socializing Agents

As children move beyond their parents' worlds, they come into contact with other agents of socialization, a variety of adults in different roles (friends' parents, coaches, youth leaders, etc.). Successful adults whose own parents were distant (physically or emotionally) or were poorly skilled at parenting often describe how a friend's parent provided the guidance and support they needed and helped them to become who they were.

Religious leaders can also serve as important agents of socialization. Most children grow up in some religious tradition, and many grow up in deeply religious families. Religious leaders—ministers, priests, rabbis, imams—can deeply influence moral socialization, but their influence can extend beyond moral development to include other types of socialization. Research by Shayne Lee, for instance, described how an influential African American church in Chicago became more committed to social and political activism under the leadership of one influential minister. This minister's presence affected not only of youth in the congregation but also older congregants. As one long-term church member told Lee, about the minister's message: "I didn't accept everything, being an older person, but I did learn a lot and I got rid of some old thinking."

Peers

One criticism of early socialization theories was that there was an undue emphasis on adults' role in socializing children. Socialization was conceptualized as a one-way process, and that meant socialization was directed from adults to children. Sociologists now recognize that peers and friends profoundly influence children's worlds, including children's behavior and values. Although parents probably remain the most influential figures in children's lives, there is no question that peers can sometimes override parental lessons.

Research on adolescents' attitudes toward and use of drugs, smoking, and drinking, for instance, reveals that peers can significantly affect a teenager's attitude and behavior. Peers also provide information that might influence attitudes on social issues in general. One study by Jerel Calzo and Monique Ward found that media and peers provided the greatest amount of information about homosexuality.

Socialization need not occur through face-to-face interactions. Arguably, social networking via Facebook or Myspace involves socialization. When your "friend" indicates her "likes," she communicates to everyone else in her network what she considers "newsworthy." Then, when a dozen more of your friends "like" this same band or television program, you're likely to check it out. In this way, peers have influenced your behavior and cultural tastes without ever talking about it face-to-face and without even knowing that they've influenced you. Future studies of peer culture and socialization are likely to pay close attention to social networking as agents of socialization.

Media

Research on media has long recognized the power of the visual or written word to shape minds. In the past, books served as a primary medium through which cultural values were communicated to children. But books, including even children's "classics," have given way to electronic forms of media. After all, children spend about one-third of their waking hours watching television, and when video and computer games are factored into this equation, the amount of time children spend with media increases tremendously (some say about 53 hours per week on average!). We review in other chapters the types of messages children (and adults) receive from media about gender, race, social class, sexuality, and so on. Our point here is that media is a powerful agent of socialization, in part because most children spend more time engaging with a form of media than in face-to-face engagements with their own parents, siblings, and friends.

One of the most dominant messages from media is that we should consume products, or rather, that we should *over*consume. That is, we are encouraged to buy things that we don't really need. As our society continues to shifts from producing goods to consuming goods, it becomes increasingly important to socialize children to be "shoppers." Here, media (especially advertisement) is undoubtedly the most influential messenger. Parents may not know the most popular toy or brand of clothing, but their children do. And these children have learned how to influence their parents' purchases, clearly demonstrating that they are (or are well on the way to becoming) socialized as consumers. Underscoring the relevance of this concept is an area of sociology devoted to understanding consumerism, including **consumer socialization,** which, according to Scott Ward, is the process "by which young people acquire skills, knowledge, and attitudes relevant to their functioning as consumers in the marketplace." We emphasize again that media is the major source of such learning. The message can be delivered through advertising, which is explicitly designed to influence consumption habits, but it can also be delivered by more subtle means, for example, "product placement" in movies and television shows. Have you ever noticed that your favorite TV show features the star drinking a popular beverage or driving a sporty car? These messages also fuel our desire to consume; perhaps on an unconscious level we believe the product will help us become like the star: beautiful, handsome, sexy, skinny, popular, and so on. Even more subtly, movies show characters engaged in a seemingly endless cycle of buying and spending as they go about their daily lives. One of our students noticed this trend:

> Every other scene was at a restaurant. The pretty, skinny people went ice-skating, carriage-riding, stayed in hotels, or went shopping. If there wasn't any shopping going on, you saw more expensive things like what they were wearing, the cell phones they were using, the cabs they were taking, or the cars they were driving. There was constant purchasing, but I didn't see much money going down.

It is probably safe to say that most media reinforce socially prescribed norms, but media is diverse and some forms and sources communicate alternative messages to children. Although rare, some children's books present interracial friendships and interactions as normal and natural. Movies such as *Shrek* provide alternative messages about the importance of women's appearance.

Toys and games

If you can imagine media as a socializing agent, perhaps you can also see how inanimate objects such as toys might be socializing influences. Researchers estimate that by the year 2012, consumer spending on toys in Europe and the United States is likely to top $122 billion. Because toys occupy a very large niche in children's lives, they also play a major role in socializing children.

Sociologists have explored the role that toys play in structuring children's play and the messages toys send about appropriate play, especially by gender (see Chapter 5 for more on the role of toys, media, and peers in gender socialization). Whether toys directly cause certain types of behavior is still debated. No one, for example, has yet come up with a definitive answer to this question: Does playing with toy guns cause children to be aggressive or are do aggressive children opt to play with guns? We can, however, safely say that toys at least reinforce certain behaviors in children. Even though children can be very creative in adapting toys designed for particular uses for their own purposes (e.g., turning a doll into an action figure), the toys that parents and adults make

Socializing agents can include electronic media. Here, a visitor at a video game show hosted by Microsoft Games Global Marketing checks out the latest games. *(Wikipedia)*

available to children to some degree structures the types of play activities that are likely to emerge. When a child is given a playhouse and miniature dishes, adventurous, rowdy play is less likely to emerge.

Toys are not just child's play, of course. Toys, especially video games, are also part of the world occupied by adolescents and adults. Research by Cathleen Zick shows that over the past few decades, adolescents have significantly reduced the amount of time they spend in paid employment while increasing time spent in leisure activities such as playing video games. Games intended for older persons also reinforce cultural messages about race, nationality, and gender.

Although toy–play should be recognized as a process and sociologically significant in its own right, it can also be analyzed in terms of potential outcomes and lessons it teaches. Toys and play can be viewed as anticipatory socialization for adult roles. When girls are encouraged to play with dolls, they are able to practice nurturing and caretaking skills. If boys are discouraged from playing with dolls, they similarly receive important messages about what boys and men are not expected to do (take care of children). Of course, we must also recognize that boys playing with dolls is linked in society's mind to another important lesson: gender conformity. What many parents who are concerned about their sons' interest in dolls (and other girly things) likely fear is that their sons will be effeminate, or gay. As sociologists, we might ask not only whether there is any connection between the two (probably not) but why the possibly of a son being

What Video Games Teach

Like many young adult males, 21-year old David van den Berg of Florida plays the video game League of Legends. David's analysis of the gender roles in the game is as follows:

The online game League of Legends reveals clear gender roles. While there are both male and female characters in the game, the female characters are unique in that their character archetypes are only linked to the character's sexuality. Almost all female characters are represented (through costumes, backstory, or vocalizations) as either the Seductress or the Virgin, whereas male characters fall into nonsexualized archetypes such as the Sorcerer or the Knight. This contrast between male and female archetypes presented by the game serves to reinforce cultural stereotypes about the worth of the feminine. The fact that the only female characters in the game are defined in this way reinforces the idea that women are valued for their sexuality.

What images have you observed in video games? Can you think of video games that provide positive messages about minorities and women?

gay is considered so problematic. The answers to these questions reveal much more about society's views on sexuality and gender than toys and dolls.

SUMMARY

By definition, social institutions are designed to keep systems operating smoothly. Social institutions also operate in such a way that they, in effect, reproduce themselves. The key players in these institutions, or agents of socialization as discussed in this chapter, are the primary means by which the values, norms, and skills of society are taught and passed on. Parents, teachers, media, and many other key figures or players within these institutional structures, work together in various ways to ensure that children become functioning members of society.

But it is also important to keep in mind that those undergoing the process of socialization are *agents* in their own right. That is, individuals do not passively receive messages from others. They can and do interpret these messages and act accordingly, sometimes even contradicting them. In addition, messages from various socializing agents can and do vary, and at times contradict each other. Parents, for example, may counter messages children receive in schools or from the media. Who "wins out" (that is, who or what ultimately shapes the child) depends upon a number of factors.

Further Reading

Calzo, Jerel P., and Monique L. Ward. "Contributions of parents, peers, and media to attitudes toward homosexuality: Investigating sex and ethnic differences." *Journal of Homosexuality* 56 (2009): 1101–1116.

Cassell, Justine, and Henry Jenkins (eds). *From Barbie to Mortal Kombat: Gender and Computer Games.* Massachusetts Institute of Technology Press, 2000.

Doucet, Andrea. *Do Men Mother? Fathering, Care, and Domestic Responsibility.* Toronto: University of Toronto Press. 2006.

Hays, Sharon. *The Cultural Contradictions of Motherhood.* New Haven: Yale University Press. 1996.

Lee, Shayne. "The church of faith and freedom: African-American Baptists and social action." *Journal for the Scientific Study of Religion* 42 (2003): 31–42.

Martin, Karin A. "'William wants a doll. Can he have one?' Feminists, child care advisors, and gender-neutral child rearing." *Gender & Society* 19 (2005): 456–479.

Merton, Robert King. *Social Theory and Social Structure.* New York: The Free Press, 1968.

Reddy, Maureen T. *Crossing the Color Line: Race, Parenting, and Culture.* New Brunswick, N.J.: Rutgers University Press, 1994.

Stacey, Judith, and Timothy J. Biblarz. (How) "Does the sexual orientation of parents matter?" *American Sociological Review* 66 (2001): 159-183.

Ward, Scott. Consumer socialization. *Journal of Consumer Research 1 (1974):* 1-14.

CHAPTER 3

ACQUIRING SELF AND IDENTITIES

In this chapter, we explore one of the most important results of socialization: the development of self. Even though each person is unique (there is no one else in the world just like you and never will be), sociologists view the "self" as a social and interactive product. It is also probably the most basic and important outcome of socialization. It, along with your social identities, which we also explore in this chapter, enables you to engage with others and the world around you.

THE SOCIAL SELF

The **self** can be thought of as a set of physical, mental, emotional, social, and spiritual traits and attributes that gives one a sense of being unique or different from others. Much of our sociological understanding of the self and its development can be traced to the work of George Herbert Mead and the publication of *Mind, Self, and Society* (1934). Mead argued that the self arises through social interaction, social activity, and social relationships.

In Chapter 1, we emphasized how important language is within the socialization process. Nowhere is this more true than in the development of one's self. Consider, for example, how a child develops her sense of self. She must understand that she has a "name" that is distinct from the names used for other objects in her world. She must also come to understand that each of those other objects has its own name and that these objects include people. When "Sara" learns that this label refers to her (and not her brother or mother or best friend), she now

37

has a framework for incorporating ideas about herself. When her mother says "Sara, look how well you dressed yourself today!" or "What a clever girl you are, Sara!" she is acquiring information about who she is that will eventually help make up her self concept.

Sociologist Charles Cooley believed that comments and reactions from other people lead to a **looking-glass self** (i.e., mirrored self). In short, others are mirrors from which our "selves" are reflected. If others respond to us in positive ways, we develop positive self concepts. And, sadly, the opposite is also true. A child who hears few compliments (or worse, much criticism), is likely to develop a low self-image or concept. For these reasons, child development specialists believe it is critical for parents and other adults to be very aware of how they speak to young children. It can be argued that the same awareness might be applied on a larger social scale; consider, for example, how the language (including compliments and criticism) can reflect and help reproduce social inequalities.

Role Taking

Once a child has developed language and a basic sense of self, that child's world expands enormously. Little "Johnny" becomes aware of others in his world—siblings, friends, strangers, and so on. This expansiveness is also met with the realization that "Johnny" is not the center of the universe! Not everyone thinks the same way or loves him the way his parents do. As difficult as this realization may be, it is critical to becoming socialized and developing a self. Imagine a world where everyone assumed everyone else thought just like they did!

Thus, a critical step that children take in the socialization process is to learn **role taking**, the ability to see the world from others' perspectives. Part of developing one's self is understanding that you are different from everyone else. The underlying mechanism for role taking, and hence the development of the self, is something called **reflexivity**, which refers to the ability to put ourselves into others' shoes, or to imagine what it would be like to see the world from their

Compliment and Criticism

Researchers Betty Hart and Todd Risley found that by age 3, children whose parents have professional jobs have experienced on average 500,000 instances of praise and 80,000 of disapproval. In contrast, children in low-income/welfare families have experienced 75,000 instances of praise and 200,000 of disapproval. How do you think these differences will shape children's views of themselves and their ability to succeed in the world when they are adults?

point of view. As a result, we are also able to examine ourselves, to look at ourselves from the outside and imagine how others might see us.

George Herbert Mead believed that children learn to role take in two stages—play stage and game stage. He used the concept of "play" and "game" both as a metaphor for what is happening in the child's world and in a concrete sense. Mead believed that children's play was absolutely critical to socialization as such activities provide lessons to a child that few others can or do.

The first stage is the **play stage**. In the play stage, the child "plays" at something. As Mead explains:

> A child plays at being a mother, at being a teacher, at being a policeman. . . .
> He plays that he is, for instance, offering himself something, and he buys it; he
> gives a letter to himself and takes it away; he addresses himself as a parent, as
> a teacher; he arrests himself as a policeman.

In this type of play, children put their newfound language and social skills to use and play allows them to hone these critical skills. They learn, among other things, how the social world is organized around roles. Through others' reactions to play activities, they also learn how to respond and interact with others. In his book *Friendship and Peer Culture in the Early Years,* sociologist William Corsaro posits that children are also experiencing and learning about group identity and communal sharing. Furthermore, they are beginning to realize that they are different from adults and share things in common with others their own age. For Corsaro, this is fundamental socialization into the fascinating world of "peer cultures" that play such a powerful role in young people's lives.

In the play stage, activities are not highly or intensely organized. There are no clear rules that must be obeyed. It's helpful, but not necessary, for a child to understand all the other roles involved for the activity to occur. You can still play "doctor" even if the child next to you is playing "house." The **game-stage**, however, is more structured and requires a better understanding of rules and roles. According to Mead, the game involves organized social activity. In the game-stage, players have specific roles and specific expectations associated with each role. To participate in a game such as baseball or soccer, it is essential that you understand what you are expected to do and what you can expect others to do. To play a game of baseball, for example, you have to understand the concept of "teams"; of pitcher, batter and shortstop; of a double-play; and so on. At this level, **role taking** requires more abstract thinking than it did in the play-stage.

It is in this game-stage that children develop the perspective of the **generalized other**. This term refers to the attitude of the whole community. It involves the ability to understand what others do and what they expect you to do. Think about the baseball game example. You can play the game effectively only if you know where everyone else is located on the field, what their roles are in carrying out each play, and the rules of baseball. A successful game means everyone has this level of understanding and works cooperatively with others on the field.

Games do more than help us role take. They teach us important cultural values, and in the process, help develop our cultural identities. The United States is a highly **individualistic culture** where each person is expected to become independent and successful but not everyone can or does. America's organized sports are arenas within which these cultural lessons are learned. Everyone is expected to be given a fair chance, but there are clear winners and losers. When we play by these rules and accept them as "givens," we are acquiring important cultural values.

In other cultures, the rules of the game may differ. Sociologist Robert Wood compared Japanese baseball to American baseball and found that Japanese teams, while playing by the same rules as American teams, interpret some of those rules differently—that is, in a way that reflects Japan's **collectivist culture**, which emphasizes the group over the individual. In the United States, the top baseball players are celebrated, and their accomplishments are praised. Players, in fact, are expected to distinguish themselves from others in terms of skills. In Japan, individual achievement is downplayed. The team, not the individual, gets credit. Woods noted that it is not unusual for Japanese game to end in a tie; nobody loses "face." Coaches may pull their power hitters from the lineup even when bases are loaded. Such interpretations of the rules that govern the game clearly reflect and reinforce cultural values in Japan, where the individual is expected to subordinate his or her needs to those of the group.

To function in the social world, we must have an understanding of what others expect of us (the generalized other). We have to learn how to work cooperatively with others to achieve goals, but we also learn cultural values such as competitiveness. As children participate in games, they also make important self-comparisons ("I'm not as fast as Mary but I'm faster than Jill"); in this way, they acquire a stronger sense of self.

SOCIALIZATION AND IDENTITY

Identity refers to an individual's self-image or mental model of one's self. In other words, the identities you hold provide a sense of who you are. Some of these identities are based upon groups you were born into (e.g., your sex or race), others come from associations or roles you have developed over time (e.g., student, father). There is also a personal identity that evolves from a personal recognition of attributes or characteristics that distinguish you from others. For example, you might view yourself as more "on time" than your brothers and sisters and therefore see yourself as different from them because you are punctual. The characteristic of punctuality becomes part of your **personal identity**—the mental self-image you have of who you are when you compare yourself to other

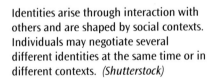

Identities arise through interaction with others and are shaped by social contexts. Individuals may negotiate several different identities at the same time or in different contexts. *(Shutterstock)*

individuals. All of these identities are part of the self, and all arise through social interaction.

Our identities shape more than our sense of self, they give rise to certain experiences and opportunities. Imagine for a moment that you are part of the Cuban-American culture. Your personal identity, or sense of self, is likely to be very different from that of a white Anglo-American teen. The diary of a young Cuban-American woman named Zulay sheds light on that difference. In the book *Red: The Next Generation of American Writers—Teenage Girls—On What Fires Up their Lives Today*, Zulay writes about a family dinner:

A family gathering at House L in Hialeah, Florida—at least twenty loud, festive Cubans and a drum set consisting of pots and pans—can be quite the scene. . . .I often skip family dinners like this. . . .But on the night of July 30th last year, my mother's birthday, something sparked within me that I would never have believed. I'd decided to join my family. We had assumed our usual seating arrangements: The elder man of the house, my father, was at the foot of the table. . . .At the far end of the table, my mother and godmother were discussing life in Cuba versus life in the U.S. . . . For the first time in eighteen years . . . I was comfortable with who I am. I was comfortable being the teenage girl with the loud Spanish-speaking, angel-collecting, too proudly Levi's-wearing family, with the pot and pan drum set.

Zulay's identity is based on a closely connected kinship system, which includes not only parents and siblings but also cousins and godparents. She is familiar with family history and stories about their lives in Cuba before they came to the United States. She speaks both English and Spanish fluently and writes in both languages about the images and colors of her life, including her mother's room-sized collection of angel statues. Zulay's identity is firmly grounded in community, family, and a keen awareness of herself as part of a social group that is different from the mainstream.

Zulay's life also reveals another important aspect of socialization and identity. Not only are we socialized to have a personal identity, the socialization process calls upon us to experience ourselves as belonging to groups and categories of people, what we call **collective identity**. Think about all the different roles you play during a single day. For example, you may be a student, a daughter, a sister, a choir member, and a soccer player. In each of these situations, different parts of yourself may be called into play. You may be very serious and studious in the classroom, but the one who can get everyone to laugh around the dinner table at night. In other words, an individual may negotiate several different identities at the same time or in different contexts.

As social beings, we have a sense of belonging to groups or collectives of other individuals. Sometimes the sense of belonging to a group may be so strong that it will seem more important than an individual's personal identity. This may occur among minority groups living in a culture when they are (or feel that they are) marginalized by the majority population. The idea of collective or group identity became especially pronounced in the United States with the rise of social movements for change in the 1970s. Much of the history of ethnic groups in the United States is a history of progressive assimilation, but during this decade in the United States, it became more common for individuals of a particular ethnicity or nationality to identify proudly with that group. For example, people of Puerto Rican ethnicity or descent in New York coined the term *Nuyorican* to emphasize their particular collective identity as Puerto Rican New Yorkers. This identity distinguished them not only from other New Yorkers but also from Puerto Ricans living on the island of Puerto Rico. The idea was that Nuyoricans had a distinct identity, which they wanted to honor. Supreme Court Justice Sonia Sotomayor considers herself a Nuyorican and has applauded the many ways that her life was shaped by her Nuyorican roots.

In sum, socialization produces in each individual a sense of self or identity. Identity might be based on individual characteristics or idiosyncrasies that seem to set us apart from others but identities also link us to others and to the larger social world by means of group affiliations. Of course, being part of a larger group or culture also requires that we know how to present ourselves in public and create certain impressions of ourselves. (Review dramaturgical theory in Volume 1 of this series for more on impression management).

Supreme Court Justice Sonia Sotomayor lauds her Nuyorican roots. *(Wikipedia)*

SUMMARY

This chapter has emphasized the social aspects of becoming human, of which the development of the self is a critical part. Sociologists argue that how individuals become a part of society is fundamentally a social process. That is, what it takes to be a social person always arises through and within social interactions. This involves, at the earliest stages, the acquisition of language and role taking skills. These skills continue to be used, and refined, as individuals grow and are socialized into new roles.

Further Reading

Cooley, Charles H. *Human Nature and Social Order.* New York: Scribner's, 1902.

Corsaro, William A. *Friendship and Peer Culture in the Early Years.* Norwood, NJ: Ablex Publishing, 1985.

Hart, Betty, and Todd Risley. "The early catastrophe: The 30 million word gap." *American Educator* 27 (2003): 4–9.

Kimmel, Michael. *Guyland: The Perilous World Where Boys Become Men.* New York: Harper, 2009.

Mead, George Herbert. *Mind, Self, & Society.* Chicago: University of Chicago Press, 1934.

Pipher, Mary. *Reviving Ophelia: Saving the Selves of Adolescent Girls.* New York: Riverhead Trade Publications, 2005.

Tatum, Beverly. *Why Are All the Black Kids Sitting Together in the Cafeteria: A Psychologist Explains the Development of Racial Identity.* New York: Basic Books, 2003.

Wood, Robert. "Samurai baseball." Source: http://www.camden.rutgers.edu/~wood/Video/vt-baseball.htm

CHAPTER 4

ACQUIRING CULTURE

INTRODUCTION

For 5,000 years, coming of age in Africa has been accompanied by traditional ceremonies initiating young people into the mysteries of adulthood. In Kenya, for example, during the month of December, young women and men may prepare themselves for a cultural "rite of passage," through which they will become full members of their societies and take on adult responsibilities. In some tribes, red ochre is prepared and applied to hair and body. Colorful beads are woven through hair and clothes. In other tribes, ghee (a clarified, semifluid butter) is used to soften and beautify the skin. Historically, these ceremonies have prepared young men for bravery and young women for early childbearing. But according to Daniel Wesangula's observation in Nairobi's *Daily Nation*, in recent years, "alternative rites of passage" have "turned culture on its head."

As Africa has become more urban, for example, the tradition of spending time alone in the bush as part of a rite of passage no longer makes sense to city boys, who listen to rap music on iPods or send text messages on cell phones. So the culture is changing to incorporate new norms—ones that still teach young people about sexuality and adult responsibility but that also guide them toward educational choices, postponing marriage, and more egalitarian gender roles. African young people respect their traditional ceremonies but they now move to the beat of the future.

Clash of cultures: Masaí warrior with a cell phone. *(Shutterstock)*

Regardless of which culture or group one belongs to, the rules, rituals, values, history and norms of that culture must be well understood. If everyone understands the rules, the group or society as a whole functions more smoothly. In turn, individuals socialized within a group feel a sense of belonging to that group, gaining an identity. The two things that emerge from this process—developing identity and knowing what it means to be a functioning member of a group—are the most fundamental outcomes of socialization. In this chapter, we explore culture and norms and why these sociological concepts are so important to our understanding of socialization.

WHAT IS CULTURE?

In 1952, Alfred Kroeber and Clyde Kluckhohn wrote a critical review of concepts of culture, which included a list of 164 different definitions of the term. Today, people still use the term to mean many different things. For example, in the humanities, "culture" might refer to art, literature, and poetry. In anthropology, the term might refer to humans' ability to use symbolic thought and might include the study of "material" culture, such as pottery, ancient ruins, or petroglyphs.

Although these definitions of the term are accurate within their own professional or academic domains, we will use the sociological definition of **culture**: the set of shared attitudes, values, goals, and practices which characterize a group, an organization, or an institution. Culture, then, is a way of life that groups of people have in common and is reflected in what they wear, what they eat, the work they do, and how they spend their leisure time. We might say that culture provides a framework within which particular groups of people organize their lives and create meaning among themselves.

We can think about cultures on a grand scale (e.g., American culture, or youth culture), but there may be distinguishable groups within these larger groups as well. Cultures within cultures are referred to as **subcultures**. For example, within "youth culture," we might find "Goths," "sk8s," "gamers," "jocks," and many other subcultures. Socialization occurs within each of these groups, just as it does within the broader culture. Members of a subculture must learn the rules, language, values, and so on, that help distinguish their group from others.

Culture as Tool Kit

Perhaps one the most helpful conceptualizations of culture comes from sociologist Ann Swidler, who defines culture as a "**tool kit**." She describes culture as a collection of resources that human actors can use for shaping **strategies for action**. Her metaphor is not only fun, it is also very useful. It is easy for us to imagine a real tool kit that we might have in the garage or carry in the car. And it is easy to conjure up a mental image of items that might be inside that tool kit.

It might hold a hammer, a tire jack, a screwdriver, and a ruler. What we find in the tool kit helps determine what we can do in a given situation. If we want to hang a picture, for example, we have a hammer and nails. If we have a flat tire, there's a jack.

Now imagine that the items in our tool kit are not just material things but are also intangibles that we carry around with us every day. For example, our tool kits might include folk tales, songs, myths, family history, symbols, poems, rituals, religious beliefs, language, jokes, and even gossip we heard yesterday at school. All of these things are there for us to choose from when we are confronted with a situation or a problem. They are the things we can draw from when we decide how we will act in any given situation. They provide us with the means to make decisions about our daily lives.

But what if certain tools are lacking? Or didn't fit? How, for example, would we deal with a flat tire if there is no jack or if the jack that is available doesn't fit? We would have to devise some other way to fix the problem. Now extend this example to something intangible, like a broken relationship. Fixing this relationship requires certain tools; if these tools are unavailable in your tool kit, you have to devise another way to solve the problem. This is precisely what we mean by saying that our cultural tool kits help us create **strategies for action**. We use the word strategies rather than behavior because it more aptly describes what goes on in a culture, which comprises many people acting individually and collectively all the time. Culture is a moving thing—it's alive, dynamic. No one tool fits every situation.

When you think about your daily life, you will realize that you don't choose your actions one at a time, evaluating each one according to your needs and interests. You can't do this because so many actions and activities are happening at the same time, in many layers of your experience. In other words, individual actions are integrated into the fabric of your day and happen almost on top of each other, maybe so fast that you can't see them. You wake up in the morning; you go to school by one means of transportation or another; you study; you interact with friends; you play games; you eat lunch or skip it; you interact

What's in Your Tool Kit?

Cuban-American Teen	Anglo-American Teen
Importance of extended family	Importance of individuality
Connection to family history/past	Connection to technology (iPod, social networking sites, mobile phone)
Community/family meals, events	Peer group associations

with teachers and school officials; you send text messages; you listen to music; you take a test. But your myriad activities are all governed by an organizing strategy—maybe you are thinking about going to college or getting married or taking your first job. The chains of activities you choose and organize are based on how you view the world. And how you view the world depends in large part on your culture and your socialization into that culture.

Imagine that you are having a major conflict with your best friend. The way you were socialized taught you to confront problems directly and immediately, before they get out of control. But your friend prefers to avoid conflict and hope it will just go away. Reaching into your tool kit, you decide to confront your friend. That strategy has worked in the past with other friends and family. Not this time, however. Your friend withdraws, or worse, starts talking about you behind your back. Now you must devise a new strategy, perhaps combining tools (direct communication, the help of a third party) to resolve the problem.

In the above example, "friendship" and what it means to be a friend, is part of one cultural tool kit or learning. But people from different countries, cultures, or groups, rely upon different tools and meanings. In some groups, for example, confronting a friend directly might be unheard of; in others, involving a third party might be considered inappropriate. Thus, people with different cultural tool kits (due to different socialization experiences) must come up with different strategies for action in similar situations. Given that your tool kit also includes subjective items among the collection of things you carry around with you, you can see that this tool kit is much more than just something to help you change a tire. In fact, it is the thing that helps you decide how to act in almost any given situation and how to interpret the actions of others.

Socialization into a culture can be thought of as the process by which an individual is provided with the basic tools from which friendships, households, and much more can be built. A society offers these tools to its members during the socializing process, along with lessons about how they are to be used and even which ones are most valuable. These tools consist of knowledge about rules and expectations, what is valued and what is not, and how to interpret a wide range of actions and situations. Once an individual has acquired a sufficient "tool kit"—that is, when she or he has been properly socialized—it becomes possible to use these tools to navigate a wide-range of situations, familiar and unfamiliar. At this point, we can view this individual as a functioning member of society and that the ultimate goal of socialization has been achieved.

NORMS, VALUES, AND SOCIAL MEANINGS

If we dig deeper into our cultural tool kit, we will find **norms**, **values** and **social meanings** or understandings. These help constitute a culture and together help define a particular group. In other words, a group (including a society or culture), can be distinguished from other groups by its norms, values, and social meanings. All these are transmitted through socialization so that members of any given culture understand how to act, think, and feel. To fully function as a member of any group or society, one must have a solid understanding of each.

Norms

Cultures are organized around approved sets of ideas and behaviors, through which a society gives "normative" support to certain ideas and behaviors. These socially approved ways of being are what sociologists call **norms**. A major outcome of socialization is learning what norms exist and what happens if someone violates one or more of these norms.

Interestingly, it's not really important and certainly not necessary for an individual to understand *why* a certain behavior is appropriate in a particular context, only what it is and when it is appropriate to display this behavior. For example, in Western society, it is the norm to greet someone you meet with a handshake. It is not important that you understand that this norm likely originated as a gesture of peace and that its original intent was to show that neither party was carrying a weapon. However, you should know when and where to shake hands (and some would argue, *how* to shake hands properly—not too hard, not too soft). You should also know when a hand shake is not appropriate. You probably wouldn't want to go around a college campus or the mall shaking everyone's hands, for instance. If you enter a different culture or geographic region, you may soon realize that other groups have different greeting norms. These might include bowing (in Asian cultures), for example, or kissing cheeks, touching noses, bringing hands together in a V-shape, or even bumping fists.

In short, meeting rituals—like all social norms—are culture-specific and vary among social groups. Unless you are socialized into a particular group, you may not know what is expected or what the gesture means. President Obama and First Lady Michelle Obama used the fist-bump greeting onstage during his Presidential campaign. This gesture, commonplace for many Americans, nevertheless attracted much public attention because it was not a norm in all segments of American culture. One Fox News anchor even questioned whether it was: "A fist bump? A pound? A terrorist fist jab?" The media attention this gesture attracted shows the disjuncture that may occur when something that is a norm among one cultural group is not understood among the general population.

As social rules, norms guide and govern people's behavior. For example, if a culture approves of aggression, and that aggression is normative and tolerated, this belief might encourage behaviors that include fighting over a sports game or settling disputes with violence. Sometimes it is difficult to define norms or to put your finger on them because they are so "normal" and taken for granted that we might not even be aware of them.

President Barack Obama and First Lady Michelle Obama bump fists during the 2008 presidential campaign. *(Getty)*

As you can see from these examples, different norms govern different cultural contexts. What might be correct in one setting or group may not be appropriate in another. Thus, socialization always is rooted in a particular social and historical context. For instance, parents are expected to teach children the social rules that apply to "eating in restaurants." But the norms governing this activity will be very different if the family is eating at McDonalds than if they are sitting in one of the city's most exclusive eating establishments. When parents teach their children proper behavior, they are usually aware of the particular expectations for a setting or a group, and this awareness becomes a critical aspect of the child's socialization.

Values

Culture is more than a set of group norms that govern our behavior. It is also how we *think* and *feel* about those behaviors. Thus, culture also includes ideas and judgments *about* behaviors, ideas, even groups of people. It includes nuanced concepts, such as outlooks, imagery, expectations, and judgments, that are particular to a community that shares them. These aspects of culture are referred to as **values**.

Values communicate to everyone what is important to the group and helps guide individual behavior. If a community values science and technology, for example, its public schools might add more science classes to the curriculum and allocate budgetary funds for computers and technological equipment. A community that values sports, however, might encourage more athletic participation by students or allocate budgetary funds for sports equipment and a new gymnasium. Obviously, to be an integral part of a group, it's important to know what is valued and what is not, so socialization always involves learning about a group's values. Once an individual understands what is valued and important (and what is not) she or he is likely to steer toward those activities that are valued and rewarded. The athlete growing up in the science-oriented community may devote less time to sports than desired if she realizes that sports bring little recognition. This example also shows that socialization experiences are *constrained* by social structure. This same athlete will have more limited opportunities to express her talents than she would if she were living in a community where sports "ruled."

Social Meanings

In addition to values and norms, even the way people assign *meaning* to situations and objects within a social context must be learned and is therefore part of socialization. We might assume that everyone knows what a hamburger is and what one does with it, but a hamburger in India, where cows are sacred, has a completely different meaning than it does to someone living in the United States.

Meanings arise within a particular context so people in different cultures may interpret situations differently. They depend on the value(s) a culture assigns to things and activities. The close tie between values and meaning can be seen in such a simple thing as eating a meal. For many Americans, eating a meal means getting quick and efficient access to food so that we have the energy to keep up with our busy schedules. A working mother, for example, might set out a quick lunch for her teenage boys, so that they can literally grab a sandwich on their way to soccer practice. What is being valued in this context is time, the efficient use of which results in the accomplishment of more activities, in this case, the ability to both eat AND participate in soccer practice.

In other cultures, meals reflect cultural values of community and group cohesion and are based on values of shared time and mutual resources. When groups of young men from Sudan immigrated to the United States to seek asylum from years of war in their home country, they were surprised by many American norms and values. Not the least of these was Americans' way of partaking of isolated meals, each family (or part of a family) creating its own meal and eating alone. To the Sudanese boys, it seemed strange that many families did not purchase food together, cook it communally, and partake of it together. Such a cultural difference sheds light on different cultural values and, hence, the different meanings eating a meal might have. Is a meal a quick way to gain basic sustenance in a busy day? Or is it a ritual of familial and community participation? The meaning depends on our values and our values depend on culture. These meanings and understandings are imparted through the socialization process.

SOCIALIZATION AND CHANGE
Socialization is never static because culture is not static. Cultures change—sometimes gradually, sometimes very dramatically—and when they do, new norms, values, forms of social interaction, and identities are created. Individuals are often faced with learning new roles, acquiring new identities, learning new ways of managing these identities, and adapting to cultural shifts.

Although cultural change can emerge from multiple sources, a close look at changes in technology can reveal how our lives are affected by cultural change and how socialization surrounding these changes must adapt to new circumstances. Our increasing use of computers, for example, has meant that we must learn a new language of sorts. Words and phrases—and the practices to which they refer, such as RAM (random access memory) or texting or tweeting—are commonplace today but neither the vocabulary, nor the technology to which it refers, even existed 50 years ago. As these changes occur, individuals are socialized into new ways of thinking and acting, and new norms and values arise. Some of these will "stick," others will not.

We can already observe norms emerging surrounding new technologies. In many high school and college classrooms, cell phones, iPhones and Blackberries must be turned off. Currently, many teachers are at a loss as to how to prevent students from interacting on Facebook or MySpace during class-time, especially if students insist that they need their laptop computers to take notes, but it is almost certain that new rules and norms surrounding the use of laptops in the classroom will start to emerge.

A more challenging problem is the phenomenon of **sexting**. A term created by combining the words "sex" and "texting," sexting describes the act of sending photographs or messages of a sexual nature (often of self or close friends) between mobile phones. A survey conducted in 2008 revealed that of 1,280 teens and young adults, at least 20 percent of the teens and 33 percent of the young adults had texted nude or semi-nude photographs of themselves via electronic mail. Before technology made such exchanges so easy (it just takes a second to push that button), sending nude or pornographic photos via mail was considered inappropriate, if not downright "creepy." Given the newness of this practice, the norms surrounding these actions are still unclear. As a result,

Technology and Socialization: New Language and New Norms

Blog	Short for Web log, a regularly updated online journal or newsletter
Biometric Identification	Method for uniquely identifying human beings through physical traits (iris scans, digital facial recognition)
Cyber-bullying	Bullying someone via social networking sites or email
Cyber-stalking	To stalk someone via the Internet
Friend/Unfriend	To add/remove a Facebook contact
Google	To search the Internet via Google search engine
Hotspot	A site that offers wireless Internet access through a local area server
Kindle	Electronic instrument for downloading and reading books
Sexting	Sending an sexually explicit or nude photo or message via mobile phone
Social networking	To interact with others via electronic media such as Facebook or MySpace
Texting	Sending verbal messages via cell phone
Tweeting	Sending messages and other information via Twitter accounts
YouTube	A video-sharing Web site
Warchalking	Already obsolete, a term to indicate the marking of cafes and other sites with unsecured, free, wireless Internet access. WiFi became so common so quickly that the term "warchalking" became obsolete in record time.
WiFi	Wireless Internet access (as at cafes, restaurants, and airports)

social institutions have intervened to control the change and to protect those who might be harmed by it. For example, in 2009, charges of child pornography were brought against six teenagers in Greensburg, Pennsylvania, after three girls allegedly sent sexually explicit photographs of themselves to three male classmates. Similarly, two Ohio teenagers were charged with contributing to the delinquency of a minor for sending or keeping on their cell phones nude photos of two 15-year-old classmates.

Technological change has been integrated into our culture bit by bit—or byte by byte. These changes can present significant socialization challenges. Many middle-aged and older Americans do not even know what "sexting" is and have no clue that their children or grandchildren might be involved in such practices. And they almost certainly would not approve if they did know about it! So how does one properly socialize a child if the values, language, and practices embraced by one group are so different from those of the other? Why would a teenager trust and accept guidance from a parent or teacher who is likely to be "clueless" about their culture? Although adults and youth often become embroiled in disagreements about these things, with each side feeling alienated from the other, the fact is that both groups share far more cultural knowledge and values than not. Socialization into a culture is about much more than technology or popular culture; it is about sharing basic understandings about how the world works or should work (e.g., that money buys things, that children should live with their families, that romantic love is desirable)—and these shared understandings can ultimately transcend differences.

WHEN CULTURES COLLIDE

By now you know that within any given culture, there are multiple subcultures and each has its own norms, values, and meanings. Sometimes these are derived directly from mainstream culture and do not conflict with that culture or with each other; at other times they do. There are also historical moments when clashes between cultures peak, and these moments present unique insights into socialization and challenges to socialization.

Sociologists have described the 1960s as a period of dramatic cultural change in the United States, when many issues—including civil rights, the Vietnam War, drugs, sexual freedom, and corruption in politics—all confronted Americans on an intimate and daily basis. At times, there seemed to be two cultures—a traditional American culture, with its norms and values based on 19th-century ideals, and a youth culture that wanted to establish new cultural norms and values. Indeed, it was a time when changes seemed to pile upon each other so quickly, it became difficult for members of the traditional culture (and even for many members of the youth culture) to relate to the changing terrain of America. The America they saw on their nightly news seemed to have no relationship to the country in which they grew up. Many people felt that the country, in the words of one social historian, was "coming apart."

The Woodstock concert, held in August 1969 in the town of Bethel, New York, is a good example of the clash of traditional and countercultures. The concert was controversial, billing itself as three days of "peace, love, and rock-and-roll." Town residents were fearful and suspicious and became anxious when concert organizers predicted that 50,000 "hippies" would descend on the town for the event. When local dairy farmer Max Yasgur agreed to let his farm be used for the event, other local residents tried to ban the concert and even resorted to boycotting Yasgur's milk products. Their protests were of no avail. The concert took place, drawing more than half a million attendees, far more than originally predicted. Local residents braced themselves for the worst. Not only did they object to hippies in their territory, they feared the potential chaos and violence that such a massive gathering might portend. Some Bethel citizens, fearing looting and riots, wanted to call in the National Guard.

The fears expressed by these residents, and felt by millions more around the country, can be better understood when we apply a socialization framework. As we discussed earlier, one of the primary goals of socialization is to instill a sense of what is right and wrong, desirable and undesirable. This tends to result in feelings of **ethnocentrism**, or the belief that one's own culture or group is superior, normal, and correct. Other cultures and practices, by contrast, may be thought to be weird, bizarre, dirty, or dangerous. We often fear what we don't understand.

But what happened at Woodstock surprised all of America. Instead of a hotbed of violent clashes, Woodstock turned out to be a meeting place where two different cultures interacted, took stock of one another, and learned from the experience. Robert Spitz, author of *Barefoot in Babylon,* describes some of what happened, citing the reaction of dairy farmer Max Yasgur to the event after it was over. Yasgur described the concert-goers as people "with music and peace on their minds." He said, "If we join them, we can turn adversities that are the problems of America today into a hope for a brighter and more peaceful future." Indeed, the Woodstock festival epitomized the fascinating ways in which American culture was being changed by the friction between traditional culture and counterculture, between young and old. It also reinforces the idea discussed earlier that members of a particular culture have far more in common with one another than not.

SUMMARY

As we've already seen, a fundamental aspect of socialization is learning about one's culture—its norms, values, and the meanings associated with various actions, ideas, and objects. It also involves acquiring a metaphorical "tool kit" that contains important cultural knowledge. The content of that tool kit will vary, depending upon what group or culture one belongs to, but what doesn't change is the importance of having one.

So learning about culture is a critical part of socialization. But culture is made up of individuals, and every one of these individuals has a sense of him or herself as a distinct individual (what sociologists call identity). Sociologists believe that the self and identity arise through socialization. Thus, you learn not only what it means to be a part of a larger group, but also what it means to be "you."

Culture is not something we are born with, nor are we born with an identity. These are not innate. Cultural traditions are transmitted from generation to generation and are learned and shared through social situations. Identities emerge through the course of these social interactions, through the process of socialization.

Thus, a major function of socialization is to instill in others a deep understanding of a culture or subculture (its norms, values, meanings) and a sense of belonging to that culture. Socialization prepares us to go through every day with a full-to-the-brim cultural tool kit, with which we make decisions. Some of these decisions reinforce cultural practices, some challenge them. In this way, culture remains fluid and changing, which further ensures that socialization is an ongoing, life-long process.

Further Reading

Anderson-Facile, Doreen. *Dueling Identities: The Christian Biker.* Lanham, Md.: Lexington Books, 2007.

Bettis, Pamela, and Natalie G. Adams (Eds). *Geographies of Girlhood: Identities in-between.* Mahwah, N.J.: Lawrence Erlbaum Associates, 2005.

Bixler, Mark. *The Lost Boys of Sudan: An American Story of the Refugee Experience.* Athens: University of Georgia Press, 2006.

Davis, Joanna R. "Growing up punk: Negotiating aging identity in a local music scene." *Symbolic Interaction* 29 (2006): 63–69.

Fadiman, Anne. *The Spirit Catches You and You Fall Down.* New York: Farrar, Straus and Giroux, 1998.

Goldwasser, Amy. *Red: The Next Generation of American Writers—Teenage Girls—on What's Firing up Their Lives Today.* New York: Hudson Street Press, 2007.

Mead, George Herbert. *Mind, Self, & Society.* Chicago: University of Chicago Press, 1934.

Spitz, Robert Stephen. *Barefoot in Babylon: The Creation of the Woodstock Music Festival, 1969.* New York: WW Norton & Co., 1989.

Swidler, Ann. "Culture in action: Symbols and strategies." *American Sociological Review* 51 (1986): 273–286.

CHAPTER 5

GENDER SOCIALIZATION

INTRODUCTION

In 2009, two parents in Sweden made international news when they announced that they had decided to keep their baby's sex a secret from everyone but a select few (e.g., those who changed the child's diapers). The child, whom they named "Pop," was two at the time and so far, the parents had succeeded at keeping their secret. Pop's outfits and hairstyles varied from feminine to masculine, depending upon Pop's moods. Pop's mother was quoted as saying "We want Pop to grow up more freely and avoid being forced into a specific gender mold from the outset. It's cruel to bring a child into the world with a blue or pink stamp on their forehead."

Not surprisingly, there was considerable outcry about this case when it hit the news. Although some applauded the parents' decision to allow their child to grow up untrammeled by rigid gender roles, others accused the parents of everything from gross stupidity to child abuse. Some child development experts argued that by not acknowledging Pop's gender, the parents were preventing the child from developing his or her own natural interests and abilities. This latter argument is interesting because if interests and abilities are in fact biologically based, or natural, they will emerge no matter how a child is raised. And Pop's parents seem okay with that too.

We suspect that Pop will reemerge in the news, perhaps upon entering school, when gender segregation is often informally and formally enforced.

Meanwhile, this case raises fascinating sociological questions and provides an interesting backdrop to some of the most important issues concerning gender socialization. Is gender based upon biological or sociological factors or both? Is it possible to change gender or is gender set early in life? What would it mean, and is it even possible, to be gender-free? Is such an outcome, even if it were possible, desirable, and what would that look like?

As earlier chapters in this volume have emphasized, socialization is the process by which individuals learn to be functioning members of society. With rare exceptions, such as for Pop discussed above, a major component of this learning is what it means to be male or female in one's particular culture. **Gender socialization** is the process through which individuals learn what it means to be male or female, masculine or feminine. Although there is much more involved in socialization than learning about gender, gender socialization is one of the most basic and pervasive socialization experiences for individuals and shapes their lives in profound ways from infancy to old age.

GENDER SOCIALIZATION IN OTHER CULTURES

One of the most important things to remember about gender socialization is that it occurs within a specific cultural and social context. What one culture expects of girls may be very different from what another culture expects. This point was made clear by Margaret Mead, the famous anthropologist who studied various cultural practices concerning gender socialization. In her book *Sex and Temperament*, Mead addresses three different cultures in New Guinea. In two of these cultures, there were very few differences between men and women. In the first, both men and women acted in ways we commonly think of as feminine—they were gentle, emotional, passive. In the second, both men and women were aggressive and distant from children (women were in fact said to dislike children). And in the third group, gender roles that our culture typically perceives as masculine or feminine were reversed. Women were dominant; men were passive and concerned about their appearance.

Cultural anthropologists have also explored cultures where more than two genders are recognized. For example, the **berdache,** or third genders, are persons in some Native American cultures (and some Southeast Asian countries) who are born into one sex but who adopt the gender of the other sex. What is important to take away from these studies by cultural anthropologists is that the outcomes of gender socialization can vary significantly across cultures. And what we assume to be normal and natural may be considered abnormal or unnatural in a different culture.

SEX AND GENDER

In thinking about the content of gender socialization, keep in mind that gender is different from sex. **Sex** refers to anatomical and biological phenomena associated with reproduction. These include **sex hormones** (estrogen, testosterone, progesterone) that govern sexual development (puberty) and reproduction; **anatomical** "equipment" (penis, vagina, breasts) that are typically used in reproduction and sexual interactions; and **sex chromosomes** (XX for female, XY for male) that are genetically encoded information that govern physical and sexual development.

In the United States, we are taught that there are two and only two sexes—male and female. But in fact, depending on how sex is measured, there are multiple sexes. For instance, there can be chromosomal variations beyond the two we commonly think of (XX for female or XY for male), including XO, XXX, XXY, XYY, or XX-male syndrome. Researchers also estimated that about 1 to 2 percent of all children born have some type of **sexual ambiguity**, biological conditions that make it difficult to determine easily whether an individual is male or female. Examples of this are boys are born with very small penises or girls born with enlarged clitorises. No matter how one attempts to measure "sex," the fact is there are multiple sexes, not just two. In the past, sexually ambiguous, or **intersexed,** individuals who did not fit clearly within one or the other sex category were usually subjected to medical treatments aimed at "correcting" their bodies and make them conform to just one sex category. In recent years, there has been greater awareness of the problems associated with such practices (e.g., the surgeries often leave individuals with little or no feeling in their penises or clitorises) and a growing movement to postpone or forego "reassignment" surgeries. In the process, our culture is beginning to recognize that sex is more variable than commonly assumed.

What we have discussed so far is an individual's sex, or sex category. This is not the same thing as **gender**, which refers to the cultural ideas and understandings concerning how persons within particular sex categories are expected to act and feel. It must be underscored that gender does not necessarily follow from one's sex. Transgender individuals, for instance, may display gender traits that are quite different from those typically associated with their biological sex.

One of the most important sociological contributions to understanding gender is that gender is a **social construction**. Whereas you are born with characteristics that identify you as one sex or another (or intersexed), you are not born with gender. All the things associated with masculinity and femininity are acquired as you move through the life cycle. This is the basis of gender socialization.

This chapter focuses on what and how we learn gender, although there is plenty of learning or socialization that involves sex and bodies. For example, we learn how private one should be about certain body parts; when, where, and how much touching of these parts is acceptable; how people feel about penis and breast sizes; and so on. Such learning also has a gender component in the sense that the answers to these questions are not necessarily the same for girls and boys.

To understand gender socialization, it is important to consider the **content** (what is actually learned), the **process** (how it is learned), and the **outcomes** (how individuals' lives and culture at large are shaped by these experiences). But what we learn from our culture about gender is not the whole story—humans acquire cultural information but also can create new or alternative "scripts." Here we must recognize that agency, an individual ability's to challenge and even reject cultural expectations, is important for understanding the limits of socialization.

CONTENT: WHAT WE LEARN ABOUT GENDER

Gender refers to the cultural understandings of what it means to be male or female, and it is these understandings or expectations that are internalized by individuals. These gender messages constitute the *content* of gender socialization. The expectations can and will vary somewhat, depending upon what qualities are valued by those who raised you or by your community. One family might believe that women should be "helpmates" and that men should be family leaders or heads of households. Another might believe that girls need to be able to take care of themselves and be independent. You would expect these two families to raise their sons and daughters somewhat differently. But there are certain aspects of gender that transcend group differences and serve as cultural ideals about how boys and girls, women and men, should look and act. These dominant cultural ideals concerning gender are referred to as **hegemonic definitions** of masculinity and femininity.

Hegemonic masculinity

At any point in time, there exists a cultural ideal of masculinity, which is known as **hegemonic masculinity**. Michael Kimmel, in his book *The History of Men*, traces the changes in masculinity ideals over time, but argues that what has remained constant is the characterization of hegemonic masculinity as "that which is not feminine." In other words, ideas about what it means to be a "real man" may change over time, but the overarching understanding is that real men are nothing like women.

So what does contemporary hegemonic masculinity look like apart from "not-female"? According to R.W. Connell, author of *Masculinities,* the hegemonic man is a risk-taker, aggressive, heterosexual, rational, and independent. It doesn't take much to find examples of Connell's concept of hegemonic masculinity—just watch some of the top box-office hits in theatres over the past few years. In *Avatar,* for example, you can find the quintessential masculine ideal in Colonel Quaritch—the tough, unemotional, aggressive, super-pumped, no-

nonsense military commander who is set on destroying anything that gets in his way.

The fact that the most "masculine" character in this movie was portrayed as military is not surprising. Even though women have been integrated into the military, it remains an institution that embodies hegemonic ideals of masculinity and as such, it's a good place to find examples of this ideal. For example, sociologist Frank Barrett studied how U.S. naval officers strive to uphold hegemonic masculine ideals by emphasizing toughness, courage, perseverance, and risk-taking. Barrett also found that recruits who don't live up to these masculine ideals are called "girls" or "pussies" or something similar (in other words, they're not "real men"). But because hegemonic masculinity is used to set men apart from women, what happens when real women enter the military and display all the traits associated with ideal masculinity?

Barrett notes that this poses a problem for male officers: "If . . . these grueling tests separate the men from the boys, what does it mean if a woman can pass them? One way that men transform this contradiction is through constructions [stories] of women as physically weak and unable to do what men do." As an example of such construction, consider the comments from a male officer in Barrett's study: "We do this fitness test—you have to hang from a bar. Some women hang there and just quit when it hurts instead of enduring the pain for 45 seconds or so. They'd just stop when it hurt. In boot camp you have to endure the pain or you go home. That's why women can't do combat."

While some women (and some men) undoubtedly do quit because what is demanded of them is too physically difficult, some women do persevere. Yet as long as the male officers believe women are weak, their hegemonic masculine ideals remain intact. As more and more women enter the military and prove capable of passing rigorous tests, it is likely that traits associated with ideal masculinity will change. Something else that serves to separate men from women will take its place.

In sum, part of gender socialization involves learning about idealized images of gender, or hegemonic masculinity. Clearly not everyone can live up to this, but the ideals remain in place so that everyone can judge themselves by somewhat consistent and accepted standards. For boys today, these ideals include independence, toughness, risk-taking, and most of all, being nothing like women.

Idealized femininity

Just as there is a cultural ideal for masculinity, there are ideas about what it takes to be a real woman. In contemporary society, this involves attractiveness, nurturing, grace, slenderness, and attracting a powerful, rich man. Just as hegemonic masculinity is glorified in many ways (especially in male-dominant institutions such as the military and in the media), so is idealized femininity.

Perhaps the most obvious example of this is the beauty pageant, where women are judged by their pose, looks, and shapes. Even very young girls compete in these arenas.

Girls learn from an early age that to be feminine they should pay attention to their bodies and looks. In *The Cult of Thinness*, sociologist Hesse-Biber reviews research on young women's dieting and notes that about 40 percent of 9 to 10-year olds say they sometimes or very often diet, that 5 to 10 million young women and girls have eating disorders, and that more than half of American women are dissatisfied with their bodies. One of the young women she interviewed (Delia) described how she learned as a young child to be concerned about her looks and weight. According to Hesse-Biber:

> Her mom, who at 45 is "beautiful, gorgeous, thin," instructed her on how to eat: "Only eat small amounts. Eat a thousand calories a day; don't overeat." My mom was never critical, like "You're fat." But one time, I went on a camping trip and I gained 4 pounds and she said, "You've got to lose weight." I mean, she watched what I ate. Like if I was going to get a piece of cake she would say, "Don't eat that."

Thus, part of the content of gender socialization for girls is to be hyperaware of their bodies and attractiveness because this is what they see is

Beauty pageant contestants in Louisiana, 1938. *(Wikipedia)*

valued in society. Girls learn to be alert to what others think about them and how they look. As another woman in Hesse-Biber's study said, "*I . . . learned from a very young age to surrender myself to other people's will, desire, and wants.*" Indeed, emphasized femininity means subverting one's own desires and looking after other people's needs first, whether those others be children, husbands, or friends.

Power and Dominance

Learning about gender involves more than simply understanding how women or men are expected to act in certain situations. Children also learn that power and privilege are more likely associated with men than women. In other words, learning about gender involves an understanding that masculinity is more highly valued than femininity. Think, for example, about the most popular sports in America and the best known teams in those sports. Did female figure-skating come immediately to mind? Or women's volleyball? For that matter, did the names of teams such as the Atlanta Dream or New York Liberty come to mind? (Both are women's professional basketball teams, by the way.)

In a college class taught by one of the authors of this volume, students were asked to imagine what it would be like if they were born someone of the other sex. The results were interesting and disturbing. All of the men wrote about what they would have to give up and the hassles they perceived women face. Not a single man wrote about what he might gain had he been born a woman. One man, in fact, wrote "I think my life would be horrible." Women, on the other hand, wrote about the greater opportunities they would have to participate in sports or in the workplace and how much easier their lives would be. These and similar answers confirmed that there is no question that an important part of gender socialization is learning and understanding that power and privilege are not equally balanced between men and women.

Heterosexuality

Sexuality and gender are not the same things but there is a strong connection between the two. Popular thinking about **sexual orientation** (whether you consider yourself to be heterosexual, bisexual, homosexual, or asexual) suggests that sexual orientation stems from both sex and gender. That is, if you are female and (therefore) feminine, you are assumed to be attracted to men; and the opposite would be true for men. But just as we've seen for sex and gender, there is not necessarily a straight (excuse the pun) connection between sex, gender, and sexual orientation. For instance, an individual who is biologically female, may be feminine but may also be attracted to women.

Despite all the possibilities stemming from variations on sex, gender, and sexual orientation, our society is nonetheless governed by a strong heterosexist norm, or **heteronormativity**—the belief that only heterosexual relationships are legitimate, normal, and healthy. This means, as sociologists Karen Martin and Emily Kazyak assert, that heterosexuality is "always assumed, expected, ordinary, and privileged." An important aspect of gender socialization involves internalizing this heteronormative belief. From an early age, children learn that romantic relationships are highly valued and complete us as human beings, but this applies only to romantic relationships between men and women. It is not unusual for preschool children to have a "boyfriend" or "girlfriend" of the opposite sex; some even perform make-believe weddings. Sociologists argue that such behavior is not a "natural" or biologically driven occurrence. Instead, it is evident that children *learn* that only heterosexual romantic relationships are acceptable and that such relationships are very highly valued. They model these behaviors as they are learning what it means to be adults. Few (if any) children model same-sex relationships, probably because same-sex marriages are much less public and even illegal in most states.

Polar Opposites

Something that we assume to be factual even though it is largely unsupported by data is the idea that men and women, boys and girls, are completely different. We certainly hear it all the time—in casual conversation and in the media (think, for example, of the best-seller *Men Are from Mars, Women Are from Venus).* Sociologist Michael Kimmel calls this belief the "interplanetary theory of gender difference." In his extensive review of the literature on gender differences, however, he finds that beyond sexual anatomy, there are far more *similarities* between males and females than differences! This includes every aspect of life, from how our brains work to our friendships.

We are not suggesting that there are no differences between women and men. We are instead positing that we are socialized to believe that males and females are completely different and to ignore the things that make men and women similar. Children are a case in point. Most parents see their boys and girls behaving differently and assume that this is a natural outcome of gender differences. They generally ignore the fact that boys and girls act pretty much the same most of the time. As Michael Messner, who observed preschool children playing soccer, noted: "In the entire . . . season of weekly games and practices, I never once saw adults point to a moment in which boy and girl soccer players were doing the same thing and exclaimed to each other, 'Look at them! They are so similar!'" Yet, the similarity of the boys and the girls was clearly evident throughout the season—kids (boys and girls alike) were "playing the game, crying over a skinned knee, scrambling enthusiastically for their snacks after the games, spacing out on a bird or a flower instead of listening to the coach at practice."

Sociologists believe that what determines behavior is not biological make-up or even gender identity but social context. So, for example, if you are male and grew up in a household with only boys, you probably were enlisted to do chores around the house that are more commonly performed by girls and women (e.g., cooking) in most households. Social context (not biology) dictated this behavior.

By now, you might be thinking, "Oh, come on! Men and women are clearly different!" And it is true that we often observe men and women performing different roles in society, and within those roles, often exhibiting different behaviors. For instance, men tend to occupy positions of power within organizations and to be more commanding or assertive in their speech and behaviors. It's easy to look at this and conclude that men are naturally more assertive and dominant, and that's why they are in these positions and acting the way they are acting. Sociologist Cynthia Epstein calls this a **deceptive distinction**—that is, the differences observed are not the result of gender but of the positions people occupy. So if you put a woman in a more powerful position, she will start talking and acting more assertively. Again, it's the social context, not gendered selves, that produce the behavior. It just looks like it's gender related because the institutions themselves are organized around gender (e.g., men are the bosses, women are the secretaries).

Variations in gender content

An important point to keep in mind is that the content of gender socialization is not static nor is it identical for everyone. What a culture considers to be important for girls and boys can differ significantly. Socialization experiences are always shaped by historical, cultural, and social forces, and this is certainly true for gender. After all, what it means to be masculine or feminine varies over time and from culture to culture. For example, if you were a girl growing up in the Dayak community of Indonesia, it would be necessary for you to be highly skilled at identifying and handling rice seeds, because this is a fundamental aspect of being female. In the United States, however, such knowledge would have little or no bearing on whether you were perceived as feminine. Even within the United States, ideas about femininity and masculinity vary and are often dictated by such things as social class, race, ethnicity, and age. In other words, what it means to be feminine or masculine varies, depending upon whether a person is rich or poor, old or young, African American or white, and so on. A concrete example concerns body image. As we saw earlier, many girls in American culture grow up believing they must be thin and are dissatisfied with their bodies because they don't seem to fit the idealized model. But African American girls are less likely than white girls to have eating disorders, they are more tolerant of what is often perceived as "too much" weight, and feel better about their bodies, even if they are heavier.

Another example of how the content of gender socialization changes over time and across cultures can be found in shifting ideas about masculinity. In

Young man from the early 20th century.
(Wikipedia)

Young man from the early 21st century.
(Shutterstock)

the past, simply having a job and being able to support one's family was the cornerstone of masculinity. Today, while it is still important for men to earn a good income, there is more emphasis on physical fitness as a measure of masculinity.

In sum, gender socialization involves learning what it means to be feminine or masculine in a particular culture or context. The content of messages about gender will vary over time, by group or context, but certain types of information and expectations concerning gender tend to be passed on from generation to generation, and in some cases even from century to century. These include notions of hegemonic masculinity, idealized femininity, power and dominance, heteronormativity, and beliefs about inherent differences. How these understandings get transmitted through the socialization process is the subject of the next section.

PROCESS: HOW WE ACQUIRE AND LEARN GENDER

There has been a long-standing interest in determining what causes gender. Remember that *gender* does not necessarily stem from *sex*. Just because a person is born male does not mean that he will be perceived or feel particularly masculine.

So does gender stem from nature (that is, in our genetic or biological make-up) or nurture (something we learn), or both? Our discussion here is not intended to resolve this issue but to explore the many social processes surrounding the ways in which gender is learned in a particular culture—that is, *socialization* into gender. Is it all learned? Maybe, maybe not. But there's no question that there is plenty of "nurture" going on.

How Learning Occurs

So *how* do children actually acquire understandings about gender? Social psychologists suggest that there are multiple processes involved in learning about gender, all of which emphasize that gender is learned, not inherent in an individual's nature. Once children have labeled themselves "girl" or "boy" (a cognitive process that occurs around the age of 3 for most children), they find themselves in a gendered world. They may be surrounded by only "gender appropriate" toys and peers and may be engaging in activities parents deem appropriate for persons of their sex (e.g., girls are much more likely to take gymnastics than boys; boys are more likely to play football or lacrosse than girls). They can also see by observing others what is appropriate for men and women. They **model** these behaviors, sometimes **role playing** gendered roles such as "mommy." Such play is anticipatory socialization for children—it allows them to "practice" skills they may need in their future roles. Responses from others—praise, ridicule, etc.—will further shape children's ideas about how men and women should look and act.

Of course, as we've discussed earlier, children are not simply passive recipients of this information. They can and do sometimes "play" with these definitions of gender, creating their own gendered selves. Michael Kimmel says it best in his book *The Gendered Society*:

> I believe that individual boys and girls become gendered—that is, we learn the "appropriate" behaviors and traits that are associated with hegemonic masculinity and exaggerated femininity, and then we each, individually, negotiate our own path in a way that feels right to us. In a sense, we each "cut our own deal" with the dominant definitions of masculinity and femininity.

Messages about how to act and look as a boy or girl are everywhere. Key socializing agents impart these lessons from day one, or even earlier! Parents, media, toys, peers, teachers, grandparents, and so on, all engage in gender socialization, even if they don't do so consciously.

Early Gender Socialization

With advances in prenatal technology, **parents** can now determine the sex of their child before the baby ever sees the light of day. This knowledge has absolutely no bearing on the child's welfare—once born, girl and boy children nurse in similar ways, eliminate waste in similar ways, need protection and near-constant care, etc. But of course the child's sex *does* matter to the parents, because it allows them to make preparations for the child—to buy "appropriate" clothing and make decisions about how to decorate the nursery. It's not that boys and girls sleep differently and therefore need different cribs, or that one has more arms than another and therefore needs different clothing. The significance of knowing a child's sex has entirely to do with gender. Even before the parents see and hold their child, they have probably already formed some critical ideas about what activities that child will enjoy in life or how aggressive or sweet the child will be. Have you ever heard parents talk about how "active" their prenatal son is and, with a visible sense of pride, declare that he's going to be a football player? Clear evidence that gender socialization starts very early!

Studies show that parents have different expectations for sons and daughters and also interact with them differently. Parents create gendered environments for girls and boys by purchasing "gender-appropriate" toys, clothing, and decorations. They enroll their children in different types of sports and activities, depending upon the child's sex. They structure different types of play and peer interactions, depending upon whether they have a girl or boy. And many parents have low tolerance for children exhibiting behaviors identified as appropriate for the other gender; almost invariably they do not want their boys acting like girls (think about why it might be seen as more acceptable for girls to be tomboys than boys to be sissies). By structuring their children's world in these ways (e.g., giving them certain types of toys, steering them into certain activities), parents set in motion a whole host of influences that continue to shape their children's lives in significant ways.

Toys and Media

By buying and exposing children to different types of **toys**, parents ensure that children acquire different skills and messages. Sociologist Cary Rankin researched products advertised on a major toy-store Web site and found major differences between the toys targeting boys and girls. She found, for example, that one of the top toys for girls ages 3-4 is the Fisher-Price Loving Family Dollhouse, which comes with a pink minivan and miniature family. Conversely,

Toys are highly gendered and serve as important socialization agents. You probably have no problem identifying which of these is the toy for boys versus for girls. *(Shutterstock)*

a popular boys' toy for this age group was Batman: The Dark Knight Punch Packing Joker (an action figure of The Joker from the film *The Dark Knight*) that came with a bazooka mounted on his shoulder. It's not hard to imagine how different the play experiences would be for children who interact with either one of these toys but not the other. Such toys are another example of anticipatory socialization (in this case, practicing housekeeping for girls and aggressiveness for boys).

Another important socialization influence in children's lives is **media**. Books, fairy tales, movies, and music aimed at children provide a constant source of information and instruction to children about what it means to be a girl or boy. Research by sociologists Liz Grauerholz and Lori Baker-Sperry, for instance, found that feminine beauty is glorified in children's classic **fairy tales** and that those tales that emphasize feminine beauty are the ones that tend to get reproduced in Disney movies and books. Grauerholz's research on children's **books** also showed that gendered messages are a mainstay in these books, although more and more show girls (but not women) as adventurous and independent, similar to how boys are portrayed in books.

Many children today spend more time watching television and movies, and playing computer games, than reading books (or having them read to them), so it is important to see what types of messages are being communicated when children engage in these activities. Studies suggest that **television** programs, because they have limited time for character development, often resort to stereotypes and that watching such programs leads children to absorb stereotypic ideas about gender. Movies also convey clear messages about gender. In particular, they teach children one of the key components of gender: heteronormativity. Recall that heteronormativity is the belief that only heterosexual relationship are legitimate and normal, a belief that ensures heterosexual relationships will be considered better than same-sex relationships. In their research on children's movies, Martin and Kazyak found that most children's G-rated movies have strong sexual messages that reinforce heteronormative values.

But not all media is single-minded in its representations of gender and sexuality. In fact, some research suggests that children's media is where very nontraditional ideas can and do emerge. Television shows such as Nickelodeon's *Clarissa Explains It All*, features a strong girl lead and promotes "girl power." As researcher Sarah Banet-Weiser asserts in her article "Girls Rule! Gender, Feminism, and Nickelodeon": "The images young girls and adolescents watch on Nickelodeon . . . are empowering. . . . They are diverse, and they represent a range of options and models, and in many ways these images are a refreshing and politically authorizing change from traditional images of femininity." And researcher Jeffery Dennis found many examples of homosexual content in children's television programs, such as reference to intimate same-sex relationships, jokes that require a basic understanding of gay culture, or scenes that seem to imply that two same-sex individuals are attracted to one another.

Peers and Gender Socialization

Parents, toys, and media certainly play important roles in teaching children about gender, but as we all know, friends and peers can sometimes exert more influence than all these other sources combined. Consider the following story by Michael Messner, which is taken from his book *Taking the Field* and describes the power of peers to teach us about gender:

> When he was about three, following a fun day of play with the five-year-old girl next door, he enthusiastically asked me to buy him a Barbie like hers. He was gleeful when I took him to the store and bought him one. When we arrived home, his feet had barely hit the pavement getting out of the car before an eight-year-old neighbor boy laughed at and ridiculed him: "A Barbie? Don't you know that Barbie is a girl's toy?" No amount of parental intervention could counter this devastating peer-induced injunction against boys playing with Barbie. My son's pleasurable desire for Barbie appeared almost overnight to transform itself into shame and rejection. The doll ended up at the bottom of a heap of toys in the closet, and my son soon became infatuated, along with other boys in his preschool, with Ninja Turtles and Power Rangers.

This story illustrates more than just the power of peers to teach us about gender. It also reveals that part of the socialization process involves **gender policing**—the idea that others, especially peers, play a critical role in keeping everyone in line. As Michael Kimmel, author of *The Gendered Society,* writes: "Peers establish the rules and enforce them—constantly, relentlessly, and mercilessly."

You are probably familiar with a common gender policing practice—calling someone a "fag," "queer," or "gay." After conducting a study of high school students, researcher C.J. Pascoe remarked "I was amazed by the way in which the word seemed to pop uncontrollably out of boys' mouths in all kinds of situations," confirming just how prevalent and even acceptable this form of gender policing tends to be. Calling someone a "fag" is a weapon used by "gender police" to keep everyone in line.

Enforcing Gender and Violence against Nonconformists

There are, of course, far more serious examples of gender policing in which attacks go well beyond verbal taunts. Far too common are instances of harassment, and physical and sexual violence, directed against individuals who do not live up to gender expectations (watch the movie *Boys Don't Cry* for a case in point). Crimes against transgenders are common and serious enough that President Obama signed into law a hate crime law that gives legal protection to homosexual and transgender persons in the same ways it does for ethnic, religious, and racial minorities.

But the enforcement of a gender system can be much more subtle and common than hate crimes. One such method is what sociologists call **gender borderwork**, which is the practice of creating clear boundaries between boys and girls that emphasize their differences. In her studies on elementary school children, sociologist Barrie Thorne observed how boys and girls interacted with one another as well as within same-sex groups. In her book, *Gender Play*, Thorne describes how borderwork occurred on a regular basis—sometimes initiated by teachers who assigned boys and girls to different groups and had them compete with one another, and often by children themselves. Borderwork imposed by adults or children serves to reinforce the idea that girls and boys (or men and women) are polar opposites, one of the central lessons we learn in life. Interestingly, there are many times when boys and girls interact easily together, when "differences" are understated or irrelevant. But, as Thorne contends, by engaging in borderwork, differences are accentuated and reinforced, reminding children of their differences and allowing stereotyping and antagonism towards the other side to flourish.

Gender Socialization over the Life Course

A common misconception is that gender socialization occurs early in life and is completed by childhood. By then, children know their gender, make gender-

Gender borderwork: Separate entrances for boys and girls at a school in New York City. *(Wikipedia)*

appropriate choices (usually) without anyone standing over them telling them what to do, and can identify others' genders and know when they are not acting in accordance with social norms (e.g., children are likely to remark about seeing a man with a ponytail or a woman with a buzz-cut).

But gender socialization is something that occurs throughout one's lifetime. Remember that gender is a social construction, not an inherent trait. For this reason, we must continually act out our gender if we are to be perceived as masculine or feminine. As some sociologists say, we "**do gender**," meaning gender is something that must be displayed and accomplished through social interaction. Doing gender involves all the ways in which we tell the world that we're either a man or woman—by what we wear or don't wear on our bodies and faces, if we shave and where we shave, how we speak to other people, what type of car we drive, and so on. It's a constant feature of our lives, although most of us are so skilled at it that we don't give it much conscious thought.

The concept of doing gender can help us understand how gender socialization is a life-long process. We are always involved in doing gender, but what it means to be masculine or feminine changes. What it means and what it takes to be a masculine 10-year old is different from being a masculine 60-year old. The same distinction applies to the female gender. For example, because being attractive is so central to our cultural ideal of femininity, older women may feel the need to alter their bodies with plastic surgery or will dye their hair so that they continue to be perceived as feminine. Doing gender can also vary by social context. The way women do gender (that is, express their femininity) in the military is different from how they would do this on a cheerleading team. In both contexts, they are likely to try to want to be perceived as feminine, but different strategies are called for and opportunities to express femininity would differ.

Thus, gender socialization is not just for children. If you think about it, you're probably not the same type of woman or man that you were 10 or 20 years ago and have had to learn over time, in different situations, how to be and continue to be masculine or feminine (or neither). And for those individuals who change genders or seriously alter their gender (as in the case of transgender individuals), socialization into an entirely new role is required later in life.

OUTCOMES: THE REWARDS AND CONSEQUENCES OF GENDER SOCIALIZATION

Gender socialization has positive and negative outcomes for individuals and society. Most people enjoy doing gender and experience considerable satisfaction and pleasure enacting these roles. For a man, being "one of the guys" and engaging in masculine pursuits (e.g., contact sports) bestows status and allows him to bond with other men. And in heterosexual relationships, many of us derive pleasure from playing out our gender roles. Gender is such a central part of who we think we are that doing gender helps reaffirm our sense of self. Some would also argue that being gendered enables social organizations to function more smoothly. Households that have a clear gender division may operate more efficiently because it is clear what everyone's roles and tasks are.

As with all systems, however, there are also dysfunctional aspects of gender socialization. On the individual level, it is impossible to live up to the idealized images of masculinity and femininity (hegemonic masculinity and exaggerated femininity) and many of the negative outcomes may stem from individuals' attempts to do so. As we noted earlier, there is so much pressure on women and girls to be thin that they are particularly at risk of developing eating disorders such as **anorexia** and **bulimia**. A great number of preteen girls are dieting, and even those whose weight is within normal range fear getting fat. In fact, one study found that more than half of underweight adolescent girls are "extremely fearful" of being fat.

Masculinity and norms dictating what it means to be a "real man" can lead to male aggression. Although aggression can manifest itself as positive behavior (for example, within a competitive sports arena), it can also have deadly consequences for society at large. Men are overwhelmingly more violent than women. According to the U.S. Department of Justice, about 76 percent of all persons arrested were male and 82 percent of those arrested for violent crimes were male. As the sidebar on this matter shows, virtually all crimes are likely

Arrests by Sex

Offense charge	Percent male	Percent female
Total	75.5	24.5
Murder and non-negligent manslaughter	89.2	10.8
Forcible rape	98.8	1.2
Aggravated assault	78.5	21.5
Embezzlement	48.3	51.7
Weapons: carrying, possessing, etc.	92.5	7.5
Prostitution and commercialized vice	30.6	69.4
Sex offenses (except rape and prostitution)	91.5	8.5
Drunkenness	83.9	16.1
Disorderly conduct	73.8	26.2
Runaways	43.9	56.1

Source: U.S. Department of Justice, Federal Bureau of Investigation. Crime in the United States, 2008.

to be perpetrated by males. Only three crimes show females with higher arrest rates, and all three crimes can be classified as nonviolent.

Many of the violent crimes men commit are directed at other men, but women are more likely to be victimized by men as well. The vast majority of assaults on women and girls are perpetuated by men whom the women know. In fact, one of the most extensive studies conducted on violence against women (the National Violence Against Women Survey) shows that women who are victimized are much more likely to experience violence at the hands of an intimate partner (former or current spouse, or boyfriend) than by strangers or acquaintances. One study conducted by Christian Molidor and Richard Tolman found that over one-third of high school students had experienced violence in their dating relationships. Interestingly, boys were about as likely as girls to report experiencing violence, but girls were significantly more likely than boys to be victims of severe violence (e.g., punching, forced sexual activity). Consequently, girls were much more likely to be injured than boys.

Another consequence of gender socialization relates to men's and women's health. This topic has been studied extensively but a few key examples of gender differences in health will suffice in showing how health and gender are related. According to the Centers for Disease Control, men are likely to live about 5 fewer years than women (life expectancy for males is 75.2; for females, 80.4 years). At the other end of the life cycle, girls are more likely to suffer from depression than boys, perhaps because girls are often taught to internalize their anger. Girls are more likely than boys to consider or attempt suicide, but boys are four times more likely to die from suicide, in part because they choose more

Are You Being Abused?

Does the person you love threaten to hurt you or those you love? Blame you if they get so angry they become violent, then promise it won't happen again? Put you down in public? Prevent you from contacting friends and family? Force sex when you don't want to? Use any type of physical violence such as kicking or slapping?

If you answered "yes" to just one of the above questions, you're involved in an abusive relationship. Know that you're not alone and you have choices.

Get help immediately. Contact the National Domestic Violence Hotline at 1-800-799-SAFE (7233) or www.thehotline.org or the National Sexual Assault Hotline at 1-800-656-4673 or http://www.rainn.org/get-help/national-sexual-assault-hotline.

Sources: The American Congress of Obstetricians and Gynecologists. www.acog.org and U.S. Department of Health & Human Services. www.womenshealth.gov/violence/

lethal methods. Young men are much more likely to drink alcohol in excess and to die from accidents than young women. In short, with respect to health outcomes, men are at greater risk than women. Although there may be various factors contributing to these outcomes, the clear gender differences seen here most certainly stem in part from masculinity norms that encourage aggression and risk-taking.

There are many more consequences (and rewards) that are outcomes of gender socialization in our own country and across various cultures than can possibly be discussed here. Suffice it to say that researchers have noted gender differences in educational or career outcomes and options, crime patterns, family structures, and within numerous other social constructs. To explore outcomes of gender socialization further, spend some time thinking about the question raised earlier: What would your life be like if you had been born the other sex?

Further Reading

Crawley, Sara L., Lara J. Foley, and Constance L. Shehan. *Gendering Bodies.* Lanham, Md.: Rowman & Littlefield Publishers, 2008.

Davies, Sharyn Graham. *Challenging Gender Norms: Five Genders Among the Bugis in Indonesia.* Belmont, Calif.: Thomson, 2007.

Hesse-Biber, Sharlene Nagy. *The Cult of Thinness.* New York: Oxford University Press, 2007.

Ingraham, Chrys. *White Weddings: Romancing Heterosexuality in Popular Culture.* New York: Routledge, 2008.

Kimmel, Michael. *The Gendered Society.* New York: Oxford University Press, 2011.

Messner, Michael A. *Taking the Field: Women, Men, and Sports.* Minneapolis: University of Minnesota Press, 2002.

Pascoe, C.J. Dude, *You're a Fag: Masculinity and Sexuality in High School.* Berkeley, Calif.: University of California Press, 2007.

Preves, Sharon E. *Intersex and Identity: The Contested Self.* New Brunswick, N.J.: Rutgers University Press, 2005.

Thorne, Barrie. *Gender Play: Girls and Boys in School.* New Brunswick, N.J.: Rutgers University Press, 1999.

CHAPTER 6

RACE AND SOCIAL CLASS SOCIALIZATION

INTRODUCTION

In one of the opening scenes of the popular film *Crash*, a stylishly dressed couple, driving home from a cocktail party, is surprised when their car is pulled over by police officers. The husband is African American, his wife is of mixed race, and the police officers are white. The alleged offense—that the couple were making out while driving—is at first laughed off by the arrestees who, although embarrassed, attempt to chat with the officers and make light of the situation. The driver—a television producer—at first thinks it will be obvious that he and his wife are the social equals of the police and he assumes that the officers will treat them as peers. However, in this case, the officers exhibit racist attitudes because of the couple's skin color, treating the couple as though they are criminals.

There is a complicated social back-story to this scene. The husband has attained class privilege through his profession but remembers a time when he did not have it. Thus, when the police subject him to a rough body search, he does what they demand of him, putting his hands behind his head and submitting to a violent pat-down. His wife, however, who has always been a member of a privileged class, talks back to the police, an offense for which she is coarsely fondled and sexually molested by one of the officers. This complicated and disturbing scene shows how race and class can mean different things in different contexts and how our understanding of race and class socialization can have far-reaching effects on almost every aspect of our lives.

In this chapter, you will see how individuals experience racial and social class socialization and what this means for individuals in different racial and social class groups. We should note that although we discuss racial and class socialization in the same chapter, these must be viewed as distinct, albeit related, processes. Race and social class are indeed related (e.g., blacks are disproportionately poor), but there are also wealthy black women or poor working class white men in our society. It is such incongruities that give rise to situations such as that depicted in the movie *Crash*.

WHAT IS RACE/CLASS SOCIALIZATION?

In America, we pride ourselves on believing that we are all created equal. But a closer look at our society reveals that there are huge **inequalities** in our country. Some of these inequalities are based on race and social class, both of which can be determined at birth. Were you born into a wealthy family or into a poor family? Are you a member of the dominant social group or a member of a minority group? Is your skin black, white, brown, some other color, or some mixture of colors? Any of these things, alone or combined, may affect where you go to school, what political party you belong to, who your friends are, and even what you eat.

Just as with gender socialization, **race and social class socialization** doesn't take place outside of a social context, and this means that certain cultural ideas and understandings about how you are supposed to feel and act are based on your race or social position. It also means that your race and social class position affect both the content and the process of your socialization. They direct you into certain avenues of social experience and affect the kind of choices you make as your life unfolds.

Race and class socialization (and distinctions) have always been a part of our society. One example of class socialization comes from the 19th century when many working-class whites, often of Irish or middle-Europe descent, were employed by middle-class families as servants. The story concerns two schoolmates: a child from a middle-class home and a child whose mother worked as a kitchen maid in that middle-class home. One day, the two children came to the middle-class home after school. As they approached the front door, the daughter of the kitchen maid made it clear she could not enter the house this way. She had been socialized to understand that "people like her" should use only the back door to enter such a house. Even as a child, she had certain understandings that affected her interactions with her middle-class friend.

Children are socialized into cultural understandings concerning race in much the same way, learning how they are expected to act based on the color of their skin. Here again, understanding affects and changes interactions between individuals. White youth and children of color may play freely together as children. But for many children, socialization brings the realization that there is a gulf between them, that one of them has (or is being groomed to have) power and privilege and the other does not, and that race is the determining factor in all of this. Once this is realized, the once-comfortable friendship often dissipates.

Stephen Berrey studied hundreds of oral histories and memoirs of African Americans who were born and raised in rural Mississippi between 1930 and 1950. As Berrey noted, "Prior to beginning schooling, black and white children played together, seemingly with little or no recognition of racial differences or what those differences meant." When schooling began, the racial lines became obvious; with that, came feelings of inferiority and fear.

Berrey's research also showed that one major contributing factor affecting, promoting, and even solidifying this social divide appeared in an unlikely form—the school bus. White children rode to school in a bus; black children walked. With this simple fact of segregated life came the understanding of racial hierarchy both for white and black children, a fact that effectively made their easy socializing during early childhood no longer possible. James Robinson, a participant in Berrey's research project, cited the bus as the object that first made him recognize racial differences. John Johnson, another study participant, remembers that he felt disgusted when he saw the white children's bus was nearly empty and that black children walked. Clearly, the very existence of the

As these children get older, their interracial friendship may become uncomfortable and even unsustainable. *(Shutterstock)*

bus externalized and made visible the hierarchical divisions of society, dividing the children from one another and fracturing the previously easy interactions between them.

Another thing that changed as childhood ended was the relationship between black boys and white girls. In fact, it became especially important for black boys to unlearn their habits of playing with white girls in an easy or unsupervised way. According to Berrey's informants, the separation of black boys and white girls as they approached adolescence was rigidly enforced by black families, whose efforts to protect their black sons were sometimes harsh. While riding on a bus with his father, for example, a young black man named James Nix remarked that a white girl's hair was long and pretty. When they got home, Nix was whipped by his father, who felt compelled to bring home the lesson that such an innocent remark could have "tragic results." But such harshness was prompted by clear and present danger. Berrey cites the 1942 lynching of two fourteen-year-old black boys who had been seen by a passer-by playing with a white girl. The boys were charged with attempted rape—although there was no proof of this—then taken from the jail by a mob and lynched. After that, black boys (and their families) lived in fear of being accused of improper behavior around white girls or women.

SOCIALIZATION AND RACE

Race refers to the classification of human beings into groups based on various factors such as culture, language, social practice, or inherited characteristics, such as skin color. Whether you belong to the dominant or the minority group, you will be socialized into an understanding of social expectations that are dependent on your race. Sociologist David Newman argues that for white children, socialization into racial identity involves learning how to deal with the privileges that come with being white rather than defining their race. White children, for example, may take for granted that they can stroll through department stores without being suspected of shoplifting. Or they may assume (often correctly) that their future will include excellent schools, the certainty of college, and a profession at least equal to that of their parents. For them, social discrimination may be so invisible that they don't even know it exists.

For black and other minority children, however, socialization has a dualistic quality—children must learn the rules and behaviors of their own race/ethnic group and the rules of the majority white culture. Such dual socialization manifests itself in a variety of ways. Chinese American families, for example, may want to ensure that their children remember the old ways of their country of origin. They may teach Chinese customs (such as bowing in greeting or to show respect) in the home while at the same time teaching mainstream American social rules for their children to exhibit in the "white" world outside the home.

White and middle-class children may take for granted good schools and future opportunities.
(Shutterstock)

Furthermore, racial groups that have experienced discrimination in America—African Americans and Native Americans, for example—may also socialize their children to understand prejudice and to be prepared to experience it. In connection with this, they might warn their children to stay out of white neighborhoods at night, especially if those children are boys. Or they might warn them that ambling through stores at the local mall may be viewed suspiciously by white store owners and clerks. In fact, young African Americans are often wrongly suspected of or accused of shoplifting when they patronize middle-class stores. In 1988, this ubiquitous suspicion of black customers—young and old—reached such a degree that it led to a boycott of New York City stores by thousands of black consumers. According to the Christian Science Monitor, they were protesting "retailers' racist suspicion and prejudice against Black patrons." Whether black children are socialized to speak out about such discrimination or remain silent, they are certainly socialized to be prepared to encounter it in their future lives. Patricia Hill Collins has called this dual socialization a kind of "socialization for survival," something she says has long been a central feature of black mothering. Indeed, many of the instructions black mothers give their children center around how to safely interact with white people. Berrey confirms this by citing several examples:

[Maurice Lucas] was taught to answer whites with "yes, sir" and "no, sir"; Jessie Stewart was told to enter white homes through the back door; and Chris Young,

Sr., learned that he should never go to the white section of a restaurant.... Obie Clark's family . . . instructed him in how to act as a second-class citizen . . . addressing all whites with "Mister" and "Miss" and by going to the back doors of stores.

Content of Race Socialization

Learning White Privilege

Children who grow up white in America may have what scholar and activist Peggy McIntosh (who is white) called "an **invisible knapsack of privilege**." The contents of this knapsack may be seemingly little things, such as being able to buy pantyhose, make-up or band-aids labeled "flesh color" and find that they actually do match the color of your flesh (light). Privileges may also be associated with pervasive images in the media. That is, a white child may be able to turn on the television or go to the movies and find her/himself represented positively most, if not *all*, of the time. Super-heroes, as well as human ones, are often white. People who hold power—in television shows such as *The Closer* or *House*—are usually white, as are "real life" characters in local schools, hospitals, and criminal justice positions. In fact, white becomes the normal or neutral color, giving white children the tacit understanding that they have **racial transparency**. That is, whiteness is so obvious and so normal that white people's race is tantamount to invisible. Whites thus have the "privilege" of choosing whether or not to include their race as part of their conscious identity.

As a white person goes through the life course, such privilege translates into advantages that may pertain in housing, employment, educational, and financial opportunities. In short, whites experience a general sense of comfort and normalcy within society—of fitting in and being accepted (and acceptable) in almost any situation. Indeed, white children learn as they are growing up that being white is the standard of social approval.

Learning Marginality

The content of what children of color learn may be quite different. For example, these children may learn to anticipate discrimination and prejudice. Parents who have experienced discrimination at the hands of the dominant racial group are likely to warn their children about discrimination and provide them with knowledge they can use for self-protection. For example, children of color may be taught to cooperate with police to avoid violence, punishment, or jail (remember the television producer threatened with arrest in the movie *Crash*). And such instruction is not limited to the family circle. In the wake of the recent police killing of an innocent black man in the Bronx, the NAACP and other organizations published brochures and held public meetings to teach young people of color how to respond safely to the police—not speaking until spoken to, not making sudden movements, and always displaying open hands. These are lessons that white children would not need to learn; their racial socialization is likely to teach them that they may safely respond to police as trusted authority figures and protectors.

Some parents of color also teach their children to question or distrust certain overarching societal myths (for example, the American Dream) that are perceived as a given within the dominant group but may not be viable for minority groups. Black poet Langston Hughes, for example, wrote about African Americans who struggled to achieve the American dream but found it elusive. He wrote, "What happens to a dream deferred? Does it dry up like a raisin in the sun?" Black playwright Lorraine Hansberry later used Hughes' words for the title of her famous play *Raisin in the Sun,* a play about a black family struggling to achieve their dream in the face of severe oppression.

Some black families, however, not only opposed that oppression but also sought to deflect it through compensatory strategies they used with their children. William Raspberry, a syndicated columnist for *The Washington Post,* remembers that his mother knew the American Dream would be difficult for him to achieve because of his skin color. Consequently, she always "tried to build us up . . . because she knew the world was going to knock us down some . . . . " Along the same lines, it is interesting to note that the subtitle of President Barack Obama's *Audacity of Hope* is *Thoughts on Reclaiming the American Dream.*

One especially pernicious aspect of racial socialization that harms black males surfaces during their elementary school experience. It is something that can, as Ann Ferguson has remarked, "have scarring effects on future life chances." Ferguson studied a group of twenty fifth-and sixth-grade African American boys to understand how routine institutional practices in elementary school helped propel those boys into troubled futures. She recounts, for example, an incident in which a black school administrator was observing a black male child who was considered a troublemaker. "That one," the administrator remarked, "has a jail cell with his name on it." Ferguson, who was studying the process of school-labeling practices, found that black males often learn an "identity created by punishment" and are labeled very early in their lives as "bad boys" or future criminals. Indeed, the idea of the black man as fearsome criminal is one of the dominant representations of blackness in America—it not only determines how society sees black males but also how blacks see themselves. Ferguson describes one "troublemaker" child who observed the thickness of his school file of offenses and considered its weight and girth a source of pride. Lacking any other achievement, this child, while still in elementary school, was learning to take pride in his identity as a "bad boy." From this and similar observations Ferguson learned that "there are serious, long-term effects of being labeled a 'troublemaker' that substantially increase one's chances of ending up in jail." Educator Marian Wright Edelman has called this process the **"cradle to prison pipeline."**

Process of Race Socialization

When children watch the same television programs and attend the same schools, can there really be that much difference in how they are socialized just because of their race or their class? The answer is a rather unqualified "yes" and the result of this is **differential socialization.** Here it is important to remember that the race/class to which our parents belong affects not only the *content* but also the *process* of socialization. That is, the socialization process itself—the way children are reared—differs according to race and class.

How White Children Learn They Are Normal

There are many ways in which white children learn that they are good, normal, and socially acceptable. From the time they are old enough to watch children's cartoons, for example, they may see the "good" witch depicted in a sparkling white gown, while the "bad" witch is dressed in black. Indeed, in the media as well as in society at large, white people and whiteness in general are pervasively associated with goodness and cleanness—and, by extension, with truth, honor, and integrity. As they are being socialized, white children learn that they embody this "good" white quality.

As white children grow up, they continue to experience white privilege in a number of more overt ways. History books are written from a white-centered perspective and may not tell the whole story. It is rare that slavery, the Civil War, post-Civil War reconstruction, or current inner city circumstances are examined from a black point of view. Although books are now being published that include more diversity and color in our American past, it may be difficult for some whites to unlearn the stories they were originally told. In fact, there may be no incentive to unlearn them, because white people represent authority and occupy the majority of positions of honor and trust—judges, lawyers, doctors, senators—in our culture. It is, perhaps, a hopeful sign that many (often white) social justice organizations are beginning to spoof white privilege and to call white people's attention to their "invisible knapsack" of privilege.

On the other hand, black children may learn that they are marginalized, different, and even "bad" in our society. Ferguson has remarked that institutionalized practices "continue to marginalize or exclude African Americans in the economy and society through the exercise of rules and purportedly objective standards by individuals who consider themselves racially unbiased." As mentioned earlier, young black males are often labeled "troublemakers" in school. Ferguson observes:

> In the daily experience of being so named, regulated, and surveilled, access to the full resources of the school are increasingly denied as the boys are isolated in

non-academic spaces in school or banished to lounging at home or loitering on the streets. Time in the school dungeon means time lost from classroom learning . . . while removal from the classroom life begins at an early age, it is even more devastating, as human possibilities are stunted at a crucial formative period of life. Each year, the gap in skills grows wider and more handicapping . . .

At the same time, black boys may become objects of fear and distrust in the general culture. Such fears are exacerbated by the boys' negative experiences in school and/or nonattendance (voluntary or due to suspension or expulsion). They realize that their presence in shopping malls, on public transportation, and even on the street make adults, especially white adults, uneasy. These attitudes result in young black men adopting coping mechanisms to deal with the way they are seen by others. Ferguson points out that they may seek to "heighten the effect by brazenly asserting their presence. They fill up the sidewalks, occupy street corners, and invade private adult spaces." They may eventually threaten or misbehave, "displaying a power that reproduces the very stereotype of dangerous youth."

But what do black girls learn? The "discovery" that their self-perception as "good" or "bad" was often dependent on race became clear in the 1940s, with the "Doll Experiments" conducted by African-American psychologists Kenneth and Mamie Clark. In these experiments, the Clarks presented young black children with white dolls and black dolls, asking them to pick the ones they liked best. The overwhelming majority of black children selected the white dolls as the good, pretty, and preferred toys. Black dolls, on the other hand, were categorized as "ugly" or "bad." The experiment has been reprised in recent years with similar results.

What scholars have called **colorism** adds another dimension to this discussion. Colorism refers to the granting of privilege or disadvantage according to the lightness or darkness of a person's skin. Indeed, colorism applies within races as well as across them. According to participants in Berrey's study, for example, black children understood that colorism could apply within their communities, even within their own families. As one perceptive child, Hattie Love, observed, "The lighter you are, the whiter you are, the (more) power and things you had, the easier time." A similar understanding was expressed by Jamaican essayist and novelist Michelle Cliff, who's reaction to colorism eventually led to a personal revolt against it. In *Claiming the Identity They Taught Me to Despise*, Cliff wrote about how hard it was to be urged, even by one's own family members, to "pass" for white. Her light skin opened the door to privilege for Cliff, but she finally rejected that "passing" and began to reclaim what she called "a past bleached from our minds."

SOCIALIZATION AND CLASS

Social class socialization also affects our lives in powerful ways. **Social classes** are made up of people who occupy similar positions of power or privilege in a society—even in America where some of us think social classes do not exist. They most certainly do, and your class status can have a big effect on your life. Your position in the class system affects many taken-for-granted things, such as where your family spends leisure time, what your political beliefs are, how many times a year you go to the doctor, and even how long you will live. If you belong to the middle or upper class, your parents might take you on regular

(above and left) Children of working-class parents may frequent fast food chains while children from middle- and upper-class families may dine at expensive restaurants. (Shutterstock)

vacations and you might often eat at expensive restaurants. If you are the child of working-class parents, you might spend your summers near home, playing with relatives at a local pool. You might go out to eat with them, but are more likely to patronize fast-food restaurants like Wendy's or McDonald's rather than expensive restaurants.

It's easy to see how parents' social class can affect their children's access to resources, leisure activities, and social opportunities, which, as children age, may include (or not include) higher education, good housing, and profitable future jobs. Middle-class teens are likely to attend prestigious schools and have money to spend on extracurricular activities. Working-class teens are more likely to go to work after high school or, if they attend college, attend a community college near home. These differences affect children's futures dramatically in terms of how our society defines success and earning power.

But parents pass on more than opportunities and economic advantages. Parents' class standing also has an effect on the **values** and **orientations** children learn and the identities they develop as they grow up. This means that, in a very big way, social class and socialization are connected, specifically that your social class affects how you are socialized.

Content of Class Socialization

Middle-Class Knowledge

Social class affects the content of socialization. If you born into the middle class, the information passed to you through socialization may be very different from that passed to a working-class child, a premise supported by sociologist Annette Lareau and others. Not surprisingly, recent research about class socialization reveals that middle-class children learn such things as *self-direction*, *curiosity*, and *independence*. Because the content of their socialization encourages them to engage in conversation with adults, to reason their way through conflicts, and to question authority figures such as teachers, they tend to have a wider reach into the public sphere and display more confidence than working-class children. As Lareau discovered, middle-class children tend to have "greater verbal agility, larger vocabulary, more comfort with authority figures, and more familiarity with abstract concepts." She found, in fact, that middle-class children actively negotiate with parents, teachers, even doctors, to arrange daily activities and situations in ways that satisfy their own needs and even give them situational advantages. Moreover, their parents encourage them in this behavior, allowing them to ask questions and actively eliciting their opinions. Middle-class children also learn that their future success depends on such assertiveness and initiative—that being active, questioning, and self-assured is a *good* and natural thing. Consequently, middle-class children may behave boldly in situations where a working-class child may be intimidated. In a principal's office, for example, a middle-class child may speak up for her/himself. A working-class child is more likely to remain silent.

The content of middle-class socialization gives a child a sense of control over her/his destiny—a sense of being at the helm of a ship, controlling its direction. Sociologists have called this feeling of control a **sense of entitlement**, which can permeate a child's life and have a far-reaching effect on that child's future. As Lareau argues, middle-class children learn to act "on their own behalf to gain advantages." Feeling at ease with authority figures at a young age provides these children with a **transitional learning or rehearsal period**, in which adults in their environment becomes stand-ins for those they will meet in the future. Feeling comfortable at adult dinners, for example, shaking hands firmly with their parents' friends, and looking adults directly in the eye all provide distinct advantages in future employment and educational endeavors, where traits like these will be valued.

Working-Class Knowledge

Compared to middle-class children, those from the working class often learn to confirm to authority, to listen to the "boss"—whether that boss is a parent, a teacher, or a future employer. Working-class children often learn that future success depends not on being assertive but on obeying rules and on conforming to social norms. They learn very early in their lives to be neat and clean and obey the rules at home, and this knowledge generally follows them into their future school and work behavior. You may assume that these sound like good rules, ones that will lead a working-class child to future success. Well, not necessarily.

In fact, research shows that when this rule-obeying content moves out of the home and into the world of social institutions, working-class and poor children are at a distinct *disadvantage*. Instead of a sense of entitlement, they are likely to operate from a **sense of constraint** in their relationships to certain important institutions, such as school or the workplace. From this constrained position, they may be less likely to succeed in these environments and less likely to interact with authority figures to make the rules of social institutions work for them. In short, they may be disempowered in places where they *need* to be empowered. Fear may also manifest itself in various ways, as working-class parents may pass to their children a sense of intimidation when it comes to dealing with authority figures in school and beyond. Lareau found, for example, that working-class parents were unable to find a comfortable way to deal with school bullying. Instead of arranging a meeting with school faculty or administrators, one working-class mother told her daughter to "punch a boy who was pestering her in class," while other parents expressed pride when their son "beat up another boy on the playground." When conforming to social norms doesn't work, working-class parents and children are more likely to feel frustration instead of empowerment and to strike out rather than mediate. As these children grow older, lack of trust may turn into an outright sense of fear and suspicion when dealing with institutions with which they must negotiate regularly—such as the workplace, government offices, or courts.

Process of Class Socialization

Wealthy/Middle-Class Children

Sociologist Lareau has called the process by which middle-class children are socialized **concerted cultivation**. What this means is that parents seek to "cultivate" the talents, interests, and opinions of their children in a "concerted" fashion. Instead of giving orders to their children, for example, they ask questions and seek children's opinions. They encourage children to ask questions, discuss

Concerted Cultivation. *(Shutterstock)*

issues and even disagree with their parents' ideas. Often, there is no clear line between parents and children. They are relative equals and this equality translates to other adults outside the home, such as teachers, coaches, and neighbors. Middle-class parents also create social lives for their children that are replete with extracurricular activities, which are generally organized and under the control of parents. Such activities might include soccer games, piano lessons, dance classes, art classes, or special tutoring. Research shows that concerted cultivation benefits children later in life, when they translate these skills, attitudes, and institutional aplomb into advanced education or employment arenas. In other words, the *process* through which they are socialized becomes an advantage to them in later life, when they turn these skills into talents needed to acquire jobs and for career advancement.

Working-Class/Poor Children

Children of working-class or poor parents undergo a different process of socialization. Lareau has called this the **accomplishment of natural growth**. For working-class families, she points out, the "crucial responsibilities of parenthood do not lie in eliciting their children's feelings, opinions, and thoughts." Instead, she asserts, parents sustain children's natural growth and view this process itself as an accomplishment. Moreover, there is a clear line between children and adults, with adults often issuing orders or directives instead of eliciting opinions. Because parents do not seek to control or orchestrate their children's social and after-school lives, working-class children have more control over their leisure activities. They may, in fact, enjoy long stretches of leisure time alone or with other children but *without* parental supervision. Instead of having their after-school time organized by their parents, they engage in what Lareau calls "child-initiated play." In addition, they have more contact with their extended families and kin, often seeing cousins and other relatives on a daily basis or touching base with them by phone.

If you think that this style of child socialization sounds a bit old-fashioned by contemporary standards, you may be right. It is, in very many ways, out of step with the understanding our schools and educational institutions have about child rearing today. Consequently, the child-rearing style employed by working-class parents—once taken out of the home and acted out in social institutions— appears out-of-sync with the public and professional style of schools, clubs, social situations, and, eventually, workplaces. But why? Why doesn't working-class socialization jibe with our dominant institutions and why do working-class kids, when they leave the home, find themselves at a disadvantage?

One reason is attributable to what sociologists called the **dominant set of culture repertoires**—that is, educational standards about child rearing that are currently accepted and in vogue among professionals and which permeate educational and social institutions. Dominant cultural repertoires today include the idea that talking to children is important, as is developing children's educational interests, exploring their talents, and encouraging them to be critical. Parents are encouraged to reason with children and teach them negotiating—not fist-fighting—skills. Certainly, these dominant repertoires have not always been in vogue. But they are taken for granted today. And research shows that is it middle-class parents who are able to shift their style and process of socialization more quickly than working-class parents to incorporate these repertoires as soon as they become popular. Thus, they give their children an advantage in the socialization process. So the way middle-class parents socialize their kids is often "in-sync" with current institutional styles and gives those kids with a "leg up" in the social arenas where they will eventually be educated and employed.

Working-class children, on the other hand, are socialized to feel a sense of distance and discomfort, even distrust, of institutions. Those who cannot grasp, internalize, and then teach the dominant set of cultural repertoires find both themselves and their children at a disadvantage when dealing with the world outside the home. Lareau, for example, observed working-class parents experiencing difficulty or fear dealing with children's teachers or school administrators. One mother even said that she "hated" her child's school for giving her son, as Lareau explained, "a sense of powerlessness and frustration in the face of an important institution" that he would be dealing with on a daily basis for many years of his young life.

Outcome of Race/Class Socialization

What are the consequences of race and class socialization? For one thing, differences in the process of *race* socialization may result in devastating disadvantages for young black males. As Ferguson's research showed, "Black youth are caught up in the net of the juvenile justice system at a rate of two to four times that of white youth." This would seem to indicate that young black boys are indeed, "bad boys," but evidence shows that is not the case. In their article entitled "Juvenile offenders: Prevalence, offender incidence, and arrest rates by race," researchers David Huizinga and Delbert Elliott argue that it has more to do with a socialized institutional response to black youth rather than to actual differences in behavior between white boys and black boys. They found that "there was a substantially and significantly higher risk that the minority youth would be apprehended and charged . . . by the police than the whites who reported committing the same kind of offenses." In other words, says Ferguson, "images of black male criminality and the demonization of black children play a significant role in framing actions and events in the justice system . . . "

Similarly, the process of *class* socialization may result in what sociologists call the **transmission of differential advantages**. That is, middle-class parents transmit to middle-class children the social skills through which they can cultivate social capital for the future. Certainly, middle-class kids may miss the quality time spent with extended family and kin, which is common for working-class children. Similarly, they may not be as adept at spending long stints of time alone, not having experienced the child-initiated play of their poorer counterparts. But, outside the home and in the long term, research shows that socialization through *concerted cultivation* has multiple advantages over the *accomplishment of natural growth*. By the time they are ready for the job market, middle-class youth have been socialized to fully engage the professional worlds of education and employment with confidence. Working-class youth may not be as successful in approaching education or employment in institutional settings they have been socialized to distrust and fear. The *process* of socialization, then, as well as the *content*, has lasting and profound effects on the unfolding of the lives of children from different classes.

SUMMARY

Race and class position affect the content of our socialization. White children learn white privilege, often without even realizing it. For them, the world seems open and they are taught that they can achieve the American Dream. Children of color, on the other hand, learn that our society is a more complicated and difficult terrain to negotiate because of the color of their skin. When it comes to *class*, middle-class children learn different skills and attitudes from those learned by working-class children. The former learn that they are the equals of adults and that they may question and disagree with them. They gain a sense of entitlement that accompanies them throughout their life course. Working-class children learn a sense of constraint, holding back, and even fearing social institutions that are part of their daily lives. They take these attitudes with them into their futures, which may, as a result, be more difficult or problematic.

As we saw at the beginning of this chapter, race and class socialization sometimes overlap, coincide, and "crash" into one another. Lareau's research has shown that in early life, class socialization (in both white and black children) seems to trump race in the power it has to affect a child's future possibilities. But, socialization continues over the life course and, says Lareau, race may become the more important factor as people age and confront issues such as employment, higher education, housing and, of course, traffic police. One thing is certain. Race and class socialization form the underlying fabric of our culture and are woven together in patterns both obvious and obscure. Learning about them can not only help us become better students of society but also better observers of our own possibilities and potential.

Further Reading

Berrey, Stephen A. "Resistance begins at home: The black family and lessons in survival and subversion in Jim Crow Mississippi." *Black Women, Gender and Families* 3 (2009): 65–90.

Clark, K.B. *The Dark Ghetto: Dilemmas of Social Power.* New York: Harper, 1965.

Cliff, Michelle. *Claiming the Identity They Taught Me to Despise.* New York: Persephone Press, 1980.

Collins, Patricia Hill. *Black Feminist Thought: Knowledge, Consciousness, and the Politics of Empowerment.* New York: Routledge, 2000.

Edelman, Marian Wright. *The Sea Is So Wide and My Boat Is So Small: Charting a Course for the Next Generation.* New York: Hyperion Press, 2008.

Ferguson, Ann. *Bad Boys: Public Schools in the Making of Black Masculinity.* Ann Arbor: University of Michigan Press, 2001.

Kohn, Melvin L. *Class and Conformity: A Study in Values.* Chicago: University of Chicago Press, 1977.

Lareau, Annette. *Unequal Childhoods: Class, Race, and Family Life.* Berkeley, Calif.: University of California Press, 2003.

McIntosh, Peggy. Working Paper #189. Wellesley, MA: Wellesley College Center for Research on Women, 1988.

Mills, C. Wright. *White Collar: The American Middle Classes.* New York: Oxford University Press, 1953.

Newman, Katherine F. *No Shame in My Game: The Working Poor in the Inner City.* New York: Vintage Press, 2000.

Pattillo-McCoy, Mary. *Black Picket Fences: Privilege and Peril Among the Black Middle Class.* Chicago: University of Chicago Press, 2000.

CHAPTER 7

ADULT SOCIALIZATION

INTRODUCTION

A common perception of socialization is that it involves only children, but socialization is a life-long process. In contemporary societies, it is no longer the case that individuals are raised with a set of skills that can last them a life time. In fact, most adults change careers or shift to significantly different kinds of jobs at least once over the course of their adult work lives. Each change involves learning a new language, skills, and attitudes. In other words, *socialization*. And in times of rapid social change (a situation that exists in today's world), adult socialization is almost a given. In just a few decades, for example, manual typewriters were replaced by electric typewriters, which have since been replaced by word processors. Hand written letters have been replaced by emails; long texts have given way to blogging, and so on. Such transitions obviously involved learning technical skills, but they also involved learning new variations (large and small) of the *culture* of technology. In 1980, no one knew what an emoticon or spell-checker was.

Certainly time and social change put pressure on adults to learn new skills and attitudes, but as people age, the very nature of their social roles also change. Consider the role of "student." On the surface, this might appears similar across age groups—a student is "one who studies." But being in preschool is significantly different from being in high school, and such differences grow exponentially when someone moves on to college and graduate school. Each level of "schooling" or education places new demands on students, involves learning new languages, new work ethics, and so on. In many institutions of higher learning, these differences are compounded depending on the age of the individual student (traditional vs. nontraditional).

In this chapter, we explore the ways adult socialization is similar to and different from childhood socialization, which has been the focus of previous chapters. We introduce and explore the implications of the important concepts of **resocialization** and **total institutions**. Finally, we provide two case studies of adult socialization. The illustrative case studies in this chapter provide insight about adult socialization, including insights gleaned from sociological studies.

COMPARING AND CONTRASTING ADULT SOCIALIZATION WITH CHILDHOOD SOCIALIZATION

Socialization is a fact of life, whether it impacts children or adults. But there are some key differences in the content and process of socialization between the two groups. Childhood socialization involves **primary learning**, whereas adult socialization often involves secondary or **refined learning**. For a child, every aspect of cultural learning is new. Not only must you learn the word for "milk" (in English or French or Arabic, depending upon what culture you were

The Changing Language of Students

Common terms used by					
Preschoolers	Elementary school students	High school students	College students	Graduate students	Adult learners
Naptime	Recess	Study hall	Student Union	Dissertation	Continuing education
Time out	Grade	SAT/ACT	Dorms	Thesis	Certification
Sharing	P.E.	Pep rallies	Lectures	Advisor	
	(Un) Satisfactory		All-nighters	GRE/GMAT	
				Revise and resubmit	
				Publish or perish	

born into), you also have to learn that there *is* such a thing as milk and that it differs from other liquids. In other words, everything must be learned pretty much from scratch. In contrast, adults who undergo socialization usually have an existing framework within which new learning occurs. For example, socialization into a **vegan** subculture will involve learning about substitutes for milk and probably something about the dairy industry. In this way, adult socialization generally involves *refining* knowledge, or building upon what is already understood (i.e., adults already know the word "milk" and the specific liquid it names and will focus on refining that knowledge to suit new needs).

For this reason, it could also be argued that adult socialization is less intense than childhood socialization. This, of course, is oversimplification because it can be intensely frustrating and anxiety-producing to learn new skills as an adult; on the other hand, most adult socialization has specific (and therefore limited) objectives and is not likely to be the seemingly endless and relentless process children face. In most cases, adult socialization is likely to involve only one part of a person's life, not every aspect of the individual's life, and therein lies the great difference. For example, socialization into a "doctor subculture" does not require a new physician to simultaneously learn how to be a healer, spouse, parent, friend, bicyclist, consumer, and so on. A caveat to this, however, is that many adults find that major life transitions occur in relatively close proximity to one another. Given young adult life-course trajectories, the medical school graduate may indeed find herself marrying, bearing children, making a new set of friends, and changing social class positions—all in a relatively short time period. When multiple transitions occur, stress levels increase significantly, even if the changes are good. Perhaps this should give adults a better appreciation of the stress young children face everyday!

One final difference between childhood and adult socialization is the degree of choice involved. Much childhood socialization is imposed upon the child by parents and others, and children have little choice as to whether they will be a "girl," a "sibling," or a "daughter." Indeed, much learning that occurs in childhood is innately determined. Linguists, for example, would argue that children don't have a choice whether to learn language—it is an innate ability. In adulthood, socialization is socially, rather than biologically or cognitively, driven. Certainly there are many social roles that are expected and even mandatory for younger and older adults (e.g., compulsory education laws require that you spend some time in the student role), but there is at least some choice involved. The perception and reality of choice over marriage, parenting, occupation, and so on, may be more keenly experienced in highly individualistic societies (such as the United States) than in traditional collectivist cultures. In the United States, each individual is expected to find his or her own career path, marriage partner, and so on. In more traditional societies, adults may feel that they have less choice over what type of work they pursue, whom they marry, or whether to have a family. These differences are likely to be a major source of conflict for individuals in international relationships, as exemplified in movies like *Outsourced* and *Sabah*.

The Stress Scale

Psychologists Holmes and Rahe developed a stress scale to show how ordinary events can build up and have negative effects on health. The following are some of the events considered most stressful, and therefore most detrimental to individuals' health. (Note: 100 is the maximum value.)

Death of a spouse	100
Divorce	73
Marital separation	65
Imprisonment	63
Death of a close family member	63
Personal injury or illness	53
Marriage	50
Dismissal from work	47
Marital reconciliation	45
Retirement	45
Change in health of family member	44
Pregnancy	40

The scale has also been adapted to reflect young adults' (teenagers) stressors. The items at the top of the list include:

Unwed pregnancy	100
Death of parent	100
Getting married	95
Divorce of parents	90
Acquiring a visible deformity	80
Fathering an unwed pregnancy	70
Jail sentence of parent for over one year	70
Marital separation of parents	69
Death of a brother or sister	68
Change in acceptance by peers	67

Source: http://en.wikipedia.org/wiki/Holmes_and_Rahe_stress_scale

Despite these differences between childhood and adult socialization, many of the key processes and mechanisms that operate in childhood socialization can be seen in adult socialization as well. First, socialization is fundamentally social for both groups. It occurs within and through social interaction. Second, it involves the acquisition of language. Language, as we discussed in earlier chapters, reflects a culture's values. It is not possible to be a full member of a culture if you lack knowledge of its language.

Third, both childhood and adult socialization involves mutual and reciprocal processes. In other words, socialization is never one-way or unidirectional. For example, an adult being socialized into the role of parent is also playing a role in the socialization of a child or children (and vice versa). Fourth, part of socialization for children and adults involves **anticipatory socialization**. Dating or cohabiting is the adult version of "playing house." Working a part-time job during high school allows you to practice some of the skills you will need to be a competent adult (e.g., following through on tasks, time management, handling money).

As we discussed in earlier chapters, socialization involves incorporating aspects of the larger culture into the "self" so that these aspects of culture become part of one's identity. For example, a child acquires a gender identity, a deep internalized sense of being a girl or boy. What it means to be a girl or boy is derived from the wider culture. In this way, socialization serves similar functions, whether we are talking about childhood or adulthood. From a broader perspective socialization also serves as the means through which individuals and society are linked and are mutually reinforcing. Society helps shape an individual's identity, and that individual helps reinforce existing social structures.

RESOCIALIZATION

Resocialization, in the most general sense, is the process of learning attitudes, values, and behaviors that are markedly different from those in which one was previously socialized. Resocialization typically comes with the acquisition of new roles or positions in life, as well as the loss or letting go of other previously held roles. By no means is resocialization a point-in-time event. Rather, it is a process that emerges in any circumstance in which an individual is experiencing swift and significant changes. While we may experience new socialization on a daily basis in minor ways, sociologists conceptualize resocialization as what occurs when there is a drastic change in one's life. Resocialization is experienced by people of all ages. However, most resocialization takes place during adulthood when our sense of self is more stable and our prior experiences have had a great deal of time to affect our attitudes, values, and behaviors.

Resocialization can occur as the result of voluntary or involuntary life changes. **Voluntary resocialization** (getting married, attending college) involves taking on a new role under one's own volition, and is therefore vastly different from involuntary resocialization. Under voluntary resocialization, the individual is committed to undertaking the changes at hand, and is therefore more likely to accept rather than resist the resocialization that accompanies these changes. An excellent example of adult voluntary resocialization would be a career-minded working professional going back to school and reinserting herself into college life at the age of 40. Such a drastic shift in her social environment is likely to lead to numerous abrupt shifts in her life, part of the challenge of resocialization. Many of her new peers will be half her age, and the shift from employee role to student role is likely to shake up her entire life: socially, professionally, and financially.

Involuntary resocialization (for example, being sentenced to prison, becoming disabled) results from changes that go against a person's own wishes. This type of resocialization can be much more traumatic because the individual is essentially dealt a new identity without having much (or any) say in the matter. A very simple example of adult involuntary resocialization has been occurring in and around Detroit, Michigan, for the past two decades. Scores of automobile factories have been shut down as the result of emerging foreign competitors and the decline the U.S. industrial sector. As a result, thousands of assembly-line workers and other industry professionals have found themselves jobless in a city that is experiencing an unemployment rate about three times the national rate. Lacking the requisite skills to find other, comparable employment, many of these individuals are forced to seek employment in a lower-paying field of work, go back to school to acquire new skills, or perhaps even uproot themselves and move to another part of the country in search of a new job. All of the aforementioned life changes will lead to some sort of adult involuntary resocialization. Family life, peer groups, even membership in churches and other social organizations, may be shaken up as a result of such involuntary changes.

Although involuntary resocialization can occur within the general population, it commonly takes place within the confines of what the sociologist Erving Goffman calls a total institution. According to Goffman, a **total institution** is "a place of residence and work where a large number of like-situated individuals cut off from the wider society for an appreciable period of time together lead an enclosed formally administered round of life." Some might even view a total institution as "a society within a society." The quintessential examples of total institutions are mental hospitals, the military, and prisons. Upon entering any of these settings, individuals are introduced to a world that has rules and routines that are oftentimes completely contrary to the manifold freedoms experienced in the wider society. The perception of these total institutions as microsocieties can be seen even in the language used by many patients, enlistees, and inmates when referring to the rest of society as being "on the outside." Other examples of total institutions include monasteries and boarding schools, which brings to light the fact that resocialization in total institutions can be voluntary as well.

Considering how cut-off total institutions are from the rest of society, it should come as no shock that resocialization in total institutions is radically different from other forms of socialization. For total institutions to operate, a high degree of conformity and order must be established and maintained. Goffman explains resocialization within total institutions as a two-step process. The first step, called the **mortification of the self**, is the process by which an individual is stripped of former attitudes, values, and behavioral patterns. Upon entering a mental health hospital, for instance, a patient's process of "mortification" manifests itself physically—he is issued a uniform and has few (or no) personal possession.

This process is initiated by a **degradation ceremony** during which it is communicated to the patient that the authorities (doctors, nurses, staff, etc.) are superior and patients are subordinate. A parallel (but probably less polite) degradation ceremony is experienced by new prison inmates: They are fingerprinted, stripped of their clothing and possessions, forced into a shower, given institutional uniforms, and then placed in a barren cell or holding area. The first half of this degradation ceremony is part of the "mortification of the self," while the second half of the ceremony (being given uniforms, a room assignment, etc.) are the beginning of the second step of the process—resocialization itself.

Following the initial mortification of the self, an individual is introduced to the new elements of socialization. During this second step of Goffman's two-step process, patients are essentially trained to conform to the new environment. A new set of attitudes, values, and behavioral patterns are instilled within each patient, beginning with what they wear and where they sleep, and culminating in the **routinization** of their every move. In essence, their mortification continues until each individual becomes a predictable cog in the machinery that

Insights into Total Institutions

Erving Goffman is perhaps the most widely cited sociologist who has studied the effects of living within a total institution. Most of Goffman's examples of resocialization in total institutions are based on his analysis of the moral career of the mental health patient, thoroughly explained in his 1961 book *Asylums*. At the time this book was being written and published, mental hospitals were populated primarily by *involuntary* patients. Today, most mental health patients seek treatment voluntarily and may leave a facility whenever they choose. Thus, depending on how they were admitted, mental health patients may be categorized as undergoing either voluntary or involuntary resocialization.

makes up the interworkings of the institution. Although Goffman referenced this two-step process as it relates to involuntary resocialization in total institutions, the very same process (albeit voluntary) process can be seen within the U.S. military. New recruits are given government issued clothing and shipped off to a boot camp or comparable sort of basic training site where they are stripped of their individuality and resocialized to function as a solitary unit. The process is reminiscent of the ancient Japanese proverb *"The nail that sticks up gets hammered down"*—each nail (or recruit, in this case) is hammered down until it is indistinguishable from the rest. The take-home message here is that resocialization within total institutions is intended to stamp out individuality (one's former sense of self and identity) and replace it with a collective identity.

Not surprisingly, individuals being forced to undergo involuntary resocialization often reject such socialization and opt to challenge the new rules and norms. This lack of anticipatory socialization in turn leads to tighter restrictions on and stricter supervision of patients and inmates and recruits—a cyclical interaction that ultimately binds the individual into compliance. An example of the rejection of resocialization can be seen in the classic film *One Flew over the Cuckoo's Nest* (1975) starring Jack Nicholson. In this film, a character named R.P. McMurphy (Nicholson) is admitted to a mental asylum after pretending to be insane in order to avoid work as a prison inmate. He challenges and rejects any resocialization as he attempts to "wake up" the other patients to the injustices he sees, and he directly challenges the hospital staff. Through a series of degradation ceremonies, culminating in a full frontal lobotomy, McMurphy is ultimately forced into compliance. The film introduces the viewer to many of the concepts found in this chapter and powerfully conveys the experience of undergoing involuntary resocialization in a total institution.

Another equally difficult and challenging form of resocialization takes place when someone is released from a total institution. After voluntarily serving in the military or involuntarily serving a prison sentence, individuals are almost immediately faced with the reality of having to resocialize back into the broader society. In the case of recently released ex-felons, the overarching question is whether this individual will be resocialized into old criminal ways or resocialized into a more productive existence as a law-abiding citizen. Such a question lies at the center of John H. Laub and Robert J. Sampson's work *Shared Beginnings, Divergent Lives: Delinquent Boys to Age 70.*

In order to investigate this element of adult resocialization, Laub and Sampson followed a group of boys (born in the 1930s) who had exhibited deviant behavior during their adolescence in Boston, Massachusetts. While a substantial number of the boys continued to engage in deviant and criminal behavior as adults, many others turned their lives around. Laub and Sampson set out to determine what led some of the boys to continue down a deviant path (persistence) while others set their lives straight (desistance). The salient question that guided their research asked: "If nearly all of these boys engaged in some sort of delinquent or criminal career early in their lives, why did some of them cease to engage in criminal behavior while others persisted?" The answer to this question had a lot to do with an individual's involvement with an intimate partner. Those whose resocialization involved a relationship with a committed partner who encouraged them to maintain a clean, straight lifestyle, desisted from engaging in further criminal behavior. For these men, marital attachment broke them of their old routines and resocialized them into more constructive behavior patterns. On the other hand, those who had intimate partners who were similarly engaged in destructive lifestyles, as well as those who had no romantic partner at all, more often persisted in their criminal ways.

EXPLORING ADULT SOCIALIZATION IN EVERYDAY LIFE

It is relatively easy to see how living in a total institution such as a prison or boarding school, where virtually every aspect of life is controlled, would require resocialization. Most of us are not socialized as children to know or understand how to be a prisoner or soldier, so occupation of these roles requires new and intense learning. Failure to learn the role could have serious consequences—indeed, it could be fatal.

But all of us go through less intense resocialization in another realms. Indeed, adult socialization occurs many times over the course of life. Say you move from a relatively casual romantic relationship into a serious one. You have to learn new ways of showing and receiving intimacy, resolving conflicts, establishing yourself as a couple, and so on. Later, if you marry or cohabit, a whole range of circumstances may arise that require relearning how to be a partner: You may find yourself at different times being a traditional breadwinner or homemaker or an equal economic partner; living apart from your partner for periods or even separating or divorcing; you could be widowed or remarry. You may spend some time in a heterosexual relationship and some in a same-sex partnership. In short, there are nearly endless circumstances that can arise within just one dimension of people's lives (in this example, romantic partnerships), and each transition will require new learning about how to function. Some lessons won't vary much, of course, such as knowing you should show an "appropriate" amount of affection toward someone you care deeply about, but as relationships and people change, so too do the demands for new learning, or new socialization.

In order to explore the concept of adult socialization in everyday life, we will offer glimpses into two roles: becoming a member of a Greek organization at a college or university, and becoming a professional sociologist. As you will see, each one resembles to some degree the type of socialization that occurs during early childhood. To be a sociologist or sorority sister, for example, you must acquire the language, requisite skill set, and demeanor that are part of that identity. Within this process, you will experience or encounter anticipatory socialization, agents of socialization at work, and at times, degradation ceremonies that help define who you are to be.

Going Greek

Upon entering college, many students look for opportunities to engage with and participate in extracurricular clubs and organizations as a way to truly envelope themselves in the college experience. Of all the student organizations found on a contemporary college or university campus, one of the most storied elements of student involvement is Greek Life. The term "Greek Life" refers generally to any student organization that utilizes the Greek alphabet to demonstrate and symbolize the essential elements of the organization. Greek organizations typically manifest themselves in the form of fraternities and sororities, and these organizations often have either a social or academic focus. For the purpose of this analysis, our discussion will be limited to social fraternities and sororities, which are often limited to a single sex (the membership of academic fraternities usually includes both men and women).

Greek Life is admittedly different from campus to campus, but for the most part there is a similar structure across schools. To gain new members, some Greek organizations utilize a discrete week-long recruitment period called "Rush," while others utilize a more open, in-depth form of ongoing recruitment. Regardless of which form of recruitment process is practiced, the experi-

Does this scene look familiar? If so, you most likely have been socialized within Greek culture. Notice how similarly dressed the women are—one example of how they communicate their collective identity. Each sorority member was socialized into the subculture and had to learn how to dress like other "sisters." *(Wikipedia)*

ence is both intense and time consuming. Social fraternities and sororities are notorious for requiring a great deal of investment (time, effort, and money) on the part of those who accept a bid to join. Making a choice to join a social fraternity or sorority is a conscious decision that usually initiates a cycle of anticipatory socialization. However, in the case of fraternities and sororities, there is often a disconnect between the forms of socialization an individual expects and what that individual is likely to experience upon joining the organization. This disconnect may be faulted primarily to the lackadaisical, animalistic portrayal of Greek Life seen in popular films such as *Animal House* and *Old School* and television shows like *Greek* and *College Daze*. Regardless, those who choose to join a fraternity or sorority, overtly volunteer to accept new attitudes, values, and behaviors.

One of the advantages of belonging to a fraternity or sorority is the opportunity to develop leadership skills and gain experience in a team-oriented work setting. This level of socialization often comes with tenure in the organization. As members move into their junior and senior years of college, they often hold positions that help prepare them for their post-college professional life. Leadership experience is not the only intangible gain of Greek Life. Social networking is paramount to future professional success, and Greek Life is ripe with the opportunity to develop large spheres of associates who can help in the job search. In fact, this element of adult socialization was the central purpose behind the original formation of the National Pan-Hellenic Council (NPHC). The NPHC (a council of historically African American Greek organizations) was created in 1930, a time when African American men and women faced extreme forms of employment discrimination and therefore needed a strong intragroup networking system to achieve professional success. These early roots are still evident as NPHC members typically remain active in and connected to their organizations, far more so than members of other Greek councils.

Socialization into a "house" involves learning a new language. Not only does each sorority or fraternity have its own "letters" to distinguish itself from other houses, there are symbols and gestures that are used to signal to others someone's membership within the organization. Again, we see how important language is to communication: If you don't know the "handshake," it's immediately clear that you don't belong. Even though the rules and expectations for living in a sorority or fraternity are learned as one begins to be initiated into the subculture, there has been anticipatory socialization into these roles from early childhood. It is no surprise that Greek organizations use the language of "family" (brother, little sis, etc.) to signify their connections; in many ways, early family experiences teach loyalty and the close connections that are expected of each Greek member.

Perhaps the most celebrated element of Greek Life is the level of secrecy involved. New recruits are inundated with new language, symbols, and hidden meanings that embody the mission and purpose of the organization. The learning process associated with familiarizing oneself with all of this new material is both demanding and time consuming, and it can detract from other roles such as that of "student," "romantic partner," or "employee." Early organizational socialization culminates in an initiation ceremony, the intent of which is to welcome new members into full membership (on the other end of the recruitment process, the newly initiated members become part of the group initiating next year's recruits). Some organizations use this initiation event as a degradation ceremony, known as **hazing**. Hazing is the mistreatment (even abuse) of new

Hazing

Hazing is a classic and potential lethal **degradation ceremony** that serves to communicate important aspects of the group's structure—including each member's status and power within the group—and to reinforce group values. While some hazing is relatively harmless, some practices cross the line into outright abuse. Hazing has come under close scrutiny in recent years after the deaths of numerous students who have been harmed or have died from injuries suffered during hazing. Several Greek members have been convicted in these cases, and some universities have disbanded Greek houses as a consequence of hazing or to preempt it altogether.

Students engage in a hazing ritual. *(Associated Press)*

members by more senior members, and it serves the purpose of all degradation ceremonies—to show new members that they are at the bottom of the totem pole. Although joining a Greek organization is a voluntary decision, events such as hazing add an element of involuntary resocialization to an otherwise voluntary process.

Involvement in social organizations such as fraternities and sororities can also involve reinforcing and building on values and skills acquired in primary socialization. Barbara Risman studied gender socialization within Greek organizations. She found that the Greek system "created" women with goals and desires that are aligned with traditional notions of gender, while fraternities encourage the objectification of women, strong intergroup competition, and the sense that men should provide for women. As such, the Greek system works to ensure that men and women will graduate from college with "different and complimentary social skills, goals, and gender roles." There are exceptions to this, such as the gay fraternity Delta Lambda Phi, which explicitly works to change the traditional fraternity model, and insists on equality and a hazing-free recruitment process.

Becoming a Sociologist

As is the case with most professional disciplines, the journey toward becoming a professional sociologist begins, at least formally, in graduate school. Regardless of the discipline, graduate school tends to be a humbling experience. Students who previously were at the head of their classes find themselves among a group of equally successful peers and are now expected to impress their professors, who are often seen as intimidating and difficult to please.

The best known work on becoming a sociologist is by sociologists Patricia Alder and Peter Adler. The Adlers noted that a new graduate student often feels like a "fish out of water." In addition to beginning a new program, these students may also be confronting a lifestyle change, a new locale, a move away from family/friends, and lots of general "newness." But having already attended college as undergraduates, most of these students engage in the process of **refined learning** rather than large-scale resocialization. But the graduate career of an aspiring sociologist may also be fraught with difficulties. At the least, early elements in the professionalization process are marked by a great deal of ambiguity, frustration, and second-guessing as students learn a new language, practices, and norms. In their study, for example, the Adlers noted how new graduate students in the field of sociology often feel like outsiders, lacking both confidence and self-esteem. In a sense, they engage in a process reminiscent of Goffman's mortification of the self. To become successful academicians, they must first shed some of their previously held values and behaviors. In fact, some of the graduate students interviewed by the Adlers indicated that abrasive faculty members humiliated and degraded them in ways they perceived as similar to resocialization in total institutions.

The professional socialization that takes place during these early years of a sociologist's career is essential as aspiring scholars progress from neophyte to novice to seasoned professional. Through this process, graduate students must learn how to shift from being someone who receives knowledge to someone who "creates knowledge." A major part of this transition is identifying and executing a successful research program (i.e., publishing). This process of creating knowledge requires that graduate students acquire a new skill set, as well as a great degree of personal growth. Following a series of examinations and the oral presentation of the thesis or dissertation, known as the "defense" (which probably feels like degradation ceremony to most graduate students), successful students enter into their final stages of graduate study (a thesis for master's students and a dissertation for doctoral students). After embarking on a research program, spending a few semesters in the front of the classroom as teaching assistants, and engaging in professional development (e.g., attending regional meetings, participating in conference presentations, and providing service to the institutions), the graduate students begin to solidify their identities as professional sociologists.

SUMMARY

As the examples in this chapter show, adults go through intensive resocialization at various stages of their lives. Some of these experiences may be more intense or involved than others, but it is clear that socialization occurs with most life transitions. Identity development, language acquisition, anticipatory socialization—the cornerstone of all socialization experiences—can be identified in adulthood as well as childhood.

Socialization involves learning to be someone or something (be it a rock musician or a doctor or a graduate student) and to fill identified social roles in socially appropriate ways. But this is not the endpoint. We must recognize that even well-socialized individuals sometimes "rewrite" their scripts, often adding creative twists to previously well-defined social roles. They redefine, for example, what it means to be a "girl" (as evidence by the Riot Grrrl Movement, a feminist punk movement). Such individual twists, or exercises of agency, reveal the limitations of traditional sociological approaches to socialization and the importance of broadening our thinking to include ways in which socialization can result in social change, the topics of the next chapter.

Further Reading

Adler, Patricia A., and Peter Adler. "The identity career of the graduate student: Professional socialization to academic sociology." *The American Sociologist* 36 (2005): 11–27.

Goffman, Erving. *Asylums: Essays on the Social Situation of Mental Patients and Other Inmates.* Chicago: Aldine Pub. Co, 1962.

Laub, John H., and Robert J. Sampson. *Shared Beginnings, Divergent Lives: Delinquent Boys to Age 70.* Cambridge, Mass.: Harvard University Press, 2003.

Ortiz, Steven M. "Breaking out of academic isolation: The media odyssey of a sociologist." *The American Sociologist* 38 (2007): 223–249.

Risman, Barbara J. "College women and sororities: The social construction and reaffirmation of gender roles." *Journal of Contemporary Ethnography* 11 (1982): 231–252.

Yeung, King-To, Mindy Stombler, and Renee Wharton. "Making men in gay fraternities: Resisting and reproducing multiple dimensions of hegemonic masculinity." *Gender & Society* 20 (2006): 5–31.

CHAPTER 8

SOCIALIZATION FAILURES

INTRODUCTION

In this chapter, we explore so-called **failures of socialization**. Sociologists use the term **deviance** to refer to behaviors that are different from society's norms and agreed-upon values; essentially, these are behaviors that people find unacceptable, heinous, or abnormal. From a sociological perspective, however, we are not so much concerned with *judging* deviant behavior as with understanding *how* it gets to be defined and *who* gets to make the definitions. We ask questions like: What are the consequences of deviant behavior? Are consequences different for some individuals than for others? Can deviance ever be a good thing? We'll examine these and other questions as we explore different kinds of "failed" socialization and its potential usefulness to society as a whole.

SOCIALIZATION FAILURES: A NEW PERSPECTIVE ON DEVIANCE AND SOCIAL CHANGE

In some sense, socialization is destined to "fail." No social process, even one as basic and complex as socialization, can prepare an individual for all of life's many challenges. As soon as you learn your role and part, something changes that forces you to adapt and resocialize. This is especially true in rapidly changing societies such as our own, where technology in particular has reconfigured even those aspects of society that seemed most permanent and unchanging (e.g., the printed word on paper may be a thing of the past in just a few decades).

But failed socialization can be viewed in other ways, by examining attitudes or behaviors that others find offensive or threatening or fearful. One of the most obvious examples of such "failed" socialization is crime. Some people—murderers, child molesters—defy social mores and are often ostracized, punished, or imprisoned because of their actions. Other people may completely reject the rules of successful behavior defined by our culture and retreat from society altogether. Sociologist Robert Merton (1957) defined vagrants, chronic alcoholics, and the mentally ill as people who might fall into this category of social "retreat."

But Merton also pointed out that some social deviants are actually seeking to achieve the same social norms as you and I. Merton linked crime with what he dubbed **strain theory**—the disjuncture between our socially defined understanding of success and what some members of society can achieve by legitimate means. The strain experienced by those who are unable to achieve society's version of success arises from an essential contradiction. They have been socialized to believe they should achieve the American Dream but, at the same time, they have been denied access to the means to achieve it. So, when certain social goals—a big house and a nice car—are not achievable through legitimate means, some members of society may attempt to achieve them through criminal means instead.

It is a stark and unpleasant reality that this disjuncture of goals and the means to achieve them can lead to crime in our society. Nevertheless, it is important to recognize that people who engage in crime may be motivated by the same goals as are mainstream members of society. The drug dealer on the street in a poverty-stricken neighborhood, for example, may be pursuing the same goals as the real estate agent in a high-end section of the same city. Both may yearn for the same American Dream of material success and future security. Yet one uses socially acceptable means to achieve this while the other uses the barrel of a gun. Nevertheless, from a sociological perspective, socialization has not failed for either of these individuals. In fact, it has been very successful in that it has motivated them both to pursue the goals and norms of mainstream American culture.

The sociological perspective encourages us to examine the process by which society defines and reacts to deviance. How do definitions of deviance get established and how do they change? Sociologists such as David Aday, author of *Social Control at the Margins,* have pointed out that there are three main elements to the definition of deviance that help us understand how society as a group reacts to it. First of all, norms about appropriate behavior must already exist among social groups. For example, we don't take off our clothes in public or talk to ourselves on busy street corners, at least not without attracting quite a bit of negative attention! The second element of deviance is that there must be a **violation** of these social norms. That is, someone who does talk to himself on a busy corner or likes to take off his clothes in a supermarket violates and challenges our expectations of normal, acceptable behavior. And finally, the third element of deviance is **reaction**, which can be as mild as expressing shock or making derisive statements about unacceptable behavior, or as harsh as ostracism or incarceration.

But the more interesting question is whether these people (e.g., the one who mutters to herself and the one who strips in supermarkets) and their behaviors are really examples of "failed" socialization? Perhaps not. A closer look might show that they have been quite successfully socialized—but not in the same ways that are considered "normal" in our mainstream society. Deviant cultures, which have been studied extensively by sociologists, are in fact governed by strong social norms. Those norms simply differ from those of the mainstream culture. Thus, socialization into these deviant groups has actually been highly successful—so much so that it has led the individual to deviate openly from mainstream culture and adopt a different set of values. Nudists, for example, who certainly challenge our social norms, maintain subcultures that are highly organized, as do Hare Krishna members, who persistently chant on street corners, whether they are speaking to themselves or to God.

So deviance means different things to different people and different cultures. Some sociologists in fact point out that deviance is relative—that is, as explained by John Curra, one person's violation of social norms is another's normal or even heroic act. Consider this example: In the aftermath of Hurricane Katrina, some members of the National Guard shot people who were looting stores in flood-ravaged New Orleans. Were their actions the results of successful socialization? Or were they criminal acts? And what about the looters? Were they merely robbers and burglars? Or were they simply people trying to survive the after-effects of one of the nation's greatest natural tragedies? Indeed, sociologists who view human behavior from the conflict perspective point out that our definitions of deviance are often created by people in power, by the very people whose interest it is to maintain their powerful positions. To understand this point, it is only necessary to observe how many street criminals are severely punished for their offenses and how many "white collar" criminals and corporations escape severe punishment for similar activities.

POSITIVE DEVIANCE

Sociologists have long suggested that deviance is not necessarily a bad thing. Emile Durkheim, for example, suggested that deviance as a particular *class* of behavior can actually serve a useful societal purpose. Durkheim saw crime as a natural kind of social activity, calling it "an integral part of all healthy societies." Although we don't normally see criminals as helping our society become a better place, what Durkheim had in mind was the idea that healthy societies *need* something to draw people together, to create a sense of mutuality and cohesion. When people violate social norms, they enable society to come together in reaction to the violation. That is, they enable others to see and define their own societal and moral boundaries. These boundaries can serve to create feelings of bonding and togetherness, a feeling that members of society have something in common. Durkheim believed that social organization would be impossible if it did not occasionally jostle up against acts of deviance. Sociologist Kai Erikson, in *Wayward Puritans*, has described this function of deviance: "Deviant forms of behavior, by marking the outer edges of group life, give the inner structure its special character and thus supply the framework within which the people of the group develop an orderly sense of their own cultural identity." Such bonds can focus the picture we have of ourselves by showing us who we are *not*. Thus, according to Erikson, the socially deviant individual "is not a bit of debris spun out by faulty social machinery, but a relevant figure in the community's overall division of labor."

Deviance can also lead to needed social change because deviant acts may ultimately function to persuade the larger group that social norms need to be adjusted or discarded. Indeed, history is replete with legends and stories in which deviance has led society to change for the better. Think of great spiritual leaders, such as Jesus or Gandhi, who, as social deviants, pushed society toward greater equality and justice.

Or think of America's Founding Fathers, who refused to accept the norms and values of their colonial masters and, through their deviant behavior, created a constitution and Bill of Rights that are unparalleled in their advocacy of participatory democracy.

The legend of Robin Hood is one of the most commonly-known examples in all of Western culture of an individual who engaged in deviant acts for the greater good of society. Stories about Robin Hood probably originated in 14th century England and have remained vital to the present day through poems, history, songs, novels, and films. Indeed, as a heroic "outlaw hero," Robin Hood was known for robbing from the rich to give to the poor. He was also known for his opposition

Whether mythic or real, the character of Robin Hood has come to symbolize the flaunting of unjust law for the betterment of society. *(Wikipedia)*

A group of black students, who were refused service at a luncheon counter reserved for white customers, staged a sit-down strike at the F.W. Woolworth store in Greensboro, North Carolina, 1960. *(Library of Congress)*

to state-sanctioned authority in the person of the Sheriff of Nottingham, who pursued Robin Hood relentlessly, seeking to restore the social order that Robin and his band of outlaws defied and disrupted. Implicit in these tales of outlawry and chivalry is the assumption that Robin's social deviance helped to create a more just society. By exposing unjust rules and practices—and by hailing the essential goodness of the common man—Robin Hood externalizes the central contradiction of his (and our) time. Sometimes committing a crime is a more just action than abiding by an evil law. The stories of Robin Hood and his outlaws—whether they are real historical persons or literary myths—broadens our social understanding of deviance by showing that it can lead to social improvement and a society that does not cater to the rich and powerful.

In a more recent example, the breaking of laws by civil rights protestors in the 1960s ultimately convinced members of the larger community to support civil rights and desegregation. The Greensboro Lunch Counter sit-ins are a prime example. In the 1960s, lunch counters such as those at department stores like Woolworth's were designated as "white only." Segregation in the American South prohibited blacks from sharing schools, swimming pools, restaurants, and other public spaces with their white counterparts. But in February 1960, four African American college students seated themselves at a Woolworth's counter in Greensboro, North Carolina. They asked for service and were denied. When Woolworth managers asked them to leave, they refused. They remained at the counter day after day, politely refusing to leave until they were properly served. This nonviolent resistance to an unjust law sparked a movement in which hundreds of community members, students, church-goers, and civil rights activists participated. By July, 1960, the protest had led to the desegregation of the Woolworth lunch counter and a victory for civil rights that echoed across the nation. Through their "deviant" behavior of breaking the codified law of the state, the students upheld what they considered a "higher" law and won a victory for desegregation in Greenboro. They also called society's attention to similar unjust laws in other states around the country.

Another example of using deviant behavior to galvanize public opinion can be seen in the high-profile example of the organization Greenpeace. Since the 1970s, Greenpeace has used unconventional tactics to alert and inform the public about crucial environmental issues. One of the main elements of Greenpeace's "style" is to use actions and images to symbolize ongoing environmental crises—images that take root in the minds and hearts of the general public. Greenpeace activists have climbed and hung banners from the Statue of Liberty, Mt. Rushmore, the Golden Gate Bridge, and even England's Big Ben, using these famous landmarks as backdrops for messages about climate change, rainforest destruction, air and water pollution, and nuclear waste.

Perhaps the most hauntingly powerful image that Greenpeace has successfully embedded in the public mind, however, is the image of tiny Greenpeace rafts valiantly positioning themselves between enormous whaling vessels and the free-swimming whales being hunted by the men on those vessels. This David-and-Goliath image struck deep into the American psyche. Before the advent of Greenpeace, not many Americans thought much about whales. But as Greenpeace protests continued, the image of the whale was transformed in the public mind, gaining an almost mythic and sacred quality. Scientists recorded whale sounds; famous musicians like Paul Winter recorded albums with whales as musical counterparts. School children painted posters, imploring Americans to "Save the Whales." And whale-watching gradually replaced whale-killing in many Western nations. Today, commercial whaling has—except in certain rogue countries—reached the nadir of social disapproval. A recent Greenpeace poll showed that 83 percent of Americans want President Obama to support an international moratorium on whale hunting that would apply to all nations of the world.

SOCIALIZATION AND AGENCY

As we have seen in this chapter, socialization is not simply learning a script and performing it. Instead, individuals critically assess social cues and messages, adapt them to fit their own needs or reject them altogether, and renegotiate

Greenpeace snow man balloon. Such symbols galvanize public interest in environmental issues. The activists who display them at highly visible and famous landmarks exemplify socialization "failures" who have been quite successful at changing public attitudes and cultural convictions. *(Salvatore Barbera. Wikipedia)*

their meanings. Socialization, like all social interaction, is a constant process by which social meanings are constructed and reconstructed. For some sociologists, this understanding includes all aspects of social life, including those that many would consider to be stable, or given, such as gender. Certainly it also includes more temporal aspects of social life, such as laws, customs, and mores. According to this view of social life, each individual has agency and can therefore renegotiate cultural definitions and meanings. As we have seen in this chapter, individuals can reject an unjust law and, like the Greensboro lunch counter students, ultimately *change* that law. Such acts of social deviance change society's understanding of what is appropriate behavior, challenging and pushing culture to a new set of values. In such instances, the individuals involved have not been socialization "failures"—instead, they have successfully exercised agency by rejecting certain culturally accepted ideas about what it means to be normal.

SUMMARY

We hope that reading this chapter has given you a new perspective on "socialization failures." Ultimately, we hope you recognize that all socialization is necessarily incomplete, and in some sense, it fails to prepare individuals for the ever-changing social world. On the other hand, it certainly succeeds in the most important ways—each individual who emerges from the process has a sense of who she or he is, both as a unique individual and as a member of a larger group. It also succeeds in giving us the basic skills and knowledge (the most important of which is language) to navigate highly complex social settings effectively. And for those who seek to alter society's rules and structures, through both criminal and heroic ways, socialization succeeds in showing the kinks and spaces within which social change, or deviance, can occur. Without socialization, none of this would be possible.

Further Reading

Aday, David P. *Social Control at the Margins*. Belmont, Calif.: Wadsworth, 1990.

Adler, Patricia A., and Peter Adler. *Constructions of Deviance: Social Power, Context, and Interaction*. New York: Wadsworth, 2008.

Curra, John O. *The Relativity of Deviance*. Thousand Oaks, Calif.: Pine Forge Press, 2000.

Durkheim, Emile. *Division of Labor in Society*. New York: The Free Press, [1893] 1997.

Erikson, Kai T. *Wayward Puritans: A Study in the Sociology of Deviance*. New York: Allyn & Bacon, 2004.

Gandhi, Mohandas. *The Story of My Experiments with Truth*. New York: Beacon, [1929] 1993.

Hahn, Thomas. *Robin Hood in Popular Culture: Violence, Transgression, and Justice*. New York: D.S. Brewer, 2000.

Herr, Melody. *Sitting for Equal Service: Lunch Counter Sit-ins*. New York: Twenty-First Century Books, 2010.

Thoreau, Henry David. *Civil Disobedience*. New York: Penguin, [1849] 2009.

Weyler, Rex. *Greenpeace: How a Group of Ecologists, Journalists, and Visionaries Changed the World*. New York: Rodale Books, 2004.

Wright, C.D. *One with Others: A Little Book of Her Days*. Port Townsend, Wash.: Copper Canyon Press, 2010.

CHAPTER 9

AFTERWORD

SOCIOLOGICAL APPROACHES TO UNDERSTANDING SOCIALIZATION

You may recall from Chapter 1 that traditional sociological approaches to understanding socialization stemmed from a **deterministic model**. In this view, children are viewed as "blank slates" upon which the rules of society are written. It is not hard to see where this idea came from. After all, we can see with our own eyes how the infant grows into an adult, how a baby understands nothing about how society works but, just a few decades later, can run a major corporation and interact with people from many different backgrounds. So it does appear that this baby, while growing up, has absorbed some of the most important lessons society teaches—how to cooperate with others, the importance of competition and striving for success, etc. But, in the process of becoming a successful member of society, she has also added to this mix her own unique personality (intelligence, ambition, etc.).

The deterministic model assumes that socialization is a one-way process, a "top-down" experience. It also rests on the notion that agents of socialization play the key role in socializing children. These agents of socialization, as explained in Chapter 2, often (though not always) represent powerful others (media, parents, teachers) who socialize the youngest and least powerful members of society. Parents and teachers, in particular, have the authority and explicit responsibility to teach young members of society how to be fully functional adults—by definition, to socialize them.

Thanks to existing social structures, it is virtually guaranteed that children will be socialized according to the rules of their respective cultures. This is true regardless of how incompetent a parent or teacher may be—the lessons of socialization are reinforced within all social institutions and structures the child encounters, from casual interactions on the playground to structured interactions in school or on a sport's team. Of course, not all members of society follow the rules of society, but almost all know what these rules are and understand them well enough to know how to violate them.

When socialization works well, it appears to be seamless and effortless. But as you have seen in this volume, it is in fact a complex process that requires tremendous engagement on the part of everyone involved—especially the person being socialized. Recognizing this, some sociologists have rejected the deterministic model of socialization and have embraced a new model—one that recognizes the child as an active participant in her own learning. This way of looking at socialization as an active, reciprocal process, is known as the **constructivist model**. The constructivist view of socialization sees the child as an extremely active participant in the socialization process and views the process as reciprocal rather than unilateral: Adults socialize children, but children also socialize adults.

The discussion of adult socialization in Chapter 7 reminds us that people continue to be socialized throughout the life course—learning new ideas and new skills that they will need as they move from one role into another. Thinking about socialization as a reciprocal, ongoing mutual process can also shed light on how individuals (or groups of individuals) can help reshape social institutions. For example, one city in Oregon has a "green" high school where students not only study but also practice conservation. The school building contains sustainable features such as recycled ceiling tiles and solar panels, and students take courses about the environment. They clean up and restore local wetlands, maintain a school-based recycling program, and monitor their own carbon footprints. Through their example, the students' activities have helped make conservation a norm beyond the school premises; this norm has been extended to the students' own homes and to the city at large. Following the students' lead, parents, neighbors, and community members report that they have begun recycling or have switched to green energy options. Thus students have made conservation a community norm—one which has socialized children and adults in the community and has also produced social change.

One of the fundamental differences between the deterministic and constructivist models is the recognition and emphasis they place on agency. To say that someone has agency suggests that person has control over something, free will, or choice. In the deterministic model, individuals being socialized were viewed as having little or no agency. Socialization happened to them, whether they wanted it or not. The constructivist model puts agency at the forefront. It recognizes that individuals are not simply sponges that soak up cultural messages. As the examples in Chapter 8 show, it is agency that gives rise to social change.

One criticism of the constructivist model is that it deemphasizes the role of social structure in shaping our actions. If you have ever gone against the "rules of society," you know how difficult it can be to exercise agency. Most of us try so hard not to stand out or to bring attention to ourselves as "different" from others, that we fail to exercise agency even in relatively safe settings. Consider how difficult many gays and lesbians find it to "come out" even to trusted friends. For some, it may take years or may involve a series of "baby steps" (e.g., first revealing bisexuality) before they feel comfortable enough to challenge the heteronormative culture in which they live.

Social structure is a powerful constraint. At times, it imposes physical constraints (jail or prison); more often it imposes psychological constraints, which can sometimes be just as confining as a prison cell. Our fear of others' reactions limits our choices and ability to exercise agency. In effect, we have been too well socialized! If not, we would not care so much about what others thought and we might act in more self-interested ways without concern for others' well-being. But because we understand the rules of society and what others expect of us, we have internalized the generalized other (discussed in Chapter 3) and we behave in ways that conform to cultural norms and do not seriously challenge existing social structures.

Thus, it is a fact that we exist within a social structure (a society if you will) that exerts tremendous influence over what types of interactions and meanings are likely to emerge. But some individuals step "outside the box." Some exercise agency by pushing the boundaries of cultural norms. Depending upon the context and circumstances, they may be viewed as heroes or as criminals, innovators or lunatics (see Chapter 8). From one perspective, we might consider these individuals to be socialization failures; from another, they illustrate the complex and fascinating relationship between individuals and society and that "failure" is sometimes a step along the way to changing a society for the better. Understanding this relationship ultimately provides insight into our own lives—how each of us is shaped by (or capable of shaping) the world around us.

GLOSSARY

accomplishment of natural growth The process by which working-class children are socialized, with parents sustaining children's natural growth but not seeking to control or orchestrate children's social lives or talents.

agency An individual's ability to challenge and even reject cultural expectations; important for understanding the limits of socialization and social change.

agents of socialization Major groups or institutions that are considered to be highly influential in teaching people about culture and norms and who often have the explicit job of socializing others.

anatomical equipment Biological organs that are typically used in reproduction and sexual interactions.

anorexia An eating disorder characterized by a refusal to eat enough food to maintain a healthy body weight and/or an obsessive fear of gaining weight.

anticipatory socialization A process of socializing people, especially children, to acquire values and understandings that are found in the roles they will presumably enter in the future.

berdache Persons in some Native American cultures who are born into one sex but who adopt the gender of the other sex.

bulimia An eating disorder characterized by binge eating followed by purging or other forms of compensatory behavior, such as fasting, using enemas or diuretics, or overexercising.

collective identity An individual's sense of belonging to a group or collective; collective identity forms part of a person's individual identity.

collectivist culture A culture which emphasizes the group over the individual.

colorism   The granting of privilege or disadvantage according to the lightness or darkness of a person's skin.

concerted cultivation   The process by which middle-class children are socialized, in which parents seek to cultivate children's talents, interests, and opinions in a "concerted" and concentrated manner.

conflict perspective   A theoretical perspective that analyzes sources of inequality in society and ways in which power is created and maintained for the advantage of certain groups.

constructivist model of socialization   The theory that a child is an eager and active participant in her/his own socialization.

counterculture   Groups that oppose or act differently from the dominant culture.

cradle-to-prison pipeline   A phrase used by Marian Wright Edelman of the Children's Defense Fund to refer to the fact that the racial socialization of black male children in the United States greatly increases their chances of ending up in jail.

culture   A set of shared attitudes, values, goals, and practices that characterize a group, an organization, or an institution.

cultural tool kit   A collection of resources that human actors can use for shaping strategies for action.

deceptive distinction   The idea that observed gender differences are not the result of gender at all but of the position one occupies in society.

degradation ceremony   An event or series of events directed at transforming an individual's identity and lowering the status of the individual.

deterministic model of socialization   The theory that a child is a "blank slate" or "tabula rasa" whose mind is filled with cultural knowledge by adults.

deviance   Behaviors that are different from society's norms and agreed-upon values.

differential socialization   The idea that both the content and process of socialization differ depending on children's race and class position.

doing gender   The idea that gender is something that must be displayed and accomplished through social interaction; all the ways in which we tell the world that we are a man or a woman.

dominant set of cultural repertoires   Educational standards about child rearing that are currently accepted and in vogue among professionals.

emotion work   The efforts we make to bring our emotions in line with cultural expectations.

essentialized gender differences   The belief that males and females are innately, biologically different; such beliefs often support a belief in male superiority by making differences seem natural.

ethnocentrism   Making value judgments about other cultures by using one's own culture as the standard.

ethnographic research   The study of human interaction in its natural setting via participant observation and interviews.

fairy tales   Myths and stories often told to children. Those that emphasize feminine beauty are the ones most likely to be reproduced in movies, television, and books.

feral children   Children who have been raised in social isolation, cut off from almost all human interaction.

game stage   The second stage in children's learning of role taking, in which playing a game involves organized social activity; there are specific roles and specific expectations associated with each role.

gender   The cultural ideas and understandings concerning how persons within particular sex categories are supposed to act and feel.

gender borderwork   The practice of creating clear boundaries between boys and girls that emphasize their differences.

gender policing   The process by which others, especially peers, keep gendered activity within bounds that are considered normal in a society.

gender socialization   Learning what it means to be feminine or masculine in a particular culture or context.

generalized other   A perspective children develop during the game stage, which involves the ability to understand what others do and what they expect you to do. This term refers to the attitude of the whole community.

hazing   The mistreatment (even abuse) of new members of a social group by more senior members, serving the purpose of showing new members they are at the bottom of the totem pole.

hegemonic masculinity   The dominant cultural ideas about masculinity; although these change over time, they are always used to set men apart from women.

heteronormativity   The assumption that heterosexuality is the normal and taken-for-granted form of sexuality in a culture.

idealized femininity   Cultural ideas about what it takes to be a "real" woman; in contemporary society, ideal feminine characteristics include attractiveness, nurturance, grace, and thinness.

identity   The essential understanding of who we are; aspects of identity include gender, race, ethnicity, and religion.

individualistic culture   A culture in which each person is expected to become independent and successful, but also one in which everyone does not have the means to attain these goals.

intensive mothering   The increased expectation on parents, especially mothers, to provide for all of their children's needs.

interpretive reproduction   The idea that children exercise creative and innovative involvement and input into their own socialization.

intersexed   The condition in which an individual's sexual differentiation is ambiguous; individuals who do not fit clearly within one or the other primary sexual category.

invisible knapsack of privilege   A phrase coined by Peggy McIntosh to refer to the unseen and often taken-for-granted advantages that accrue to being white in America. These include the privilege of choosing whether or not to include race as part of a conscious identity.

involuntary resocialization   A form of resocialization that results from changes that go against a person's own wishes.

language   A complex set of shared and commonly understood verbal and nonverbal sounds and gestures that express ideas and feelings.

looking-glass self   The belief that others are mirrors in which our "selves" are reflected.

mortification of the self   The process by which an individual is stripped of former attitudes, values, and behavioral patterns; the first step in Goffman's two-step process for resocialization in total institutions.

norms   A socially defined standard or rule of conduct.

Nuyorican   A person of Puerto Rican descent or ethnicity living in New York.

personal identity   The mental image you have of who you are when you compare yourself with other individuals.

play stage   The first stage of children's learning of role taking, in which children put newfound language and social skills to use in play, allowing them to hone critical skills.

primary learning   A form of cultural learning in which everything is new; learning the basics of social interaction.

race and class socialization   The premise that certain cultural ideas and understandings about how you are supposed to feel and act are based on your race and class position, which affect both the content and the process of socialization.

racial transparency   A situation in which whiteness becomes the normal or neutral color in a society, giving white children the tacit understanding that they are "transparent" or that their race is invisible.

refined (secondary) learning Learning by refining knowledge, or building upon what is already understood.

reflexivity The ability to put ourselves into others' shoes, to act as they act, or to imagine what it would be like to see the world from their point of view.

resocialization The process of learning attitudes, values, and behaviors that are markedly different from those adopted when one was previously socialized.

role taking The ability to see the world from others' perspectives.

routinization The development of a regulated, predictable procedure; lacking variance or spontaneity.

self A set of physical, mental, emotional, social, and spiritual traits and attributes that produce a sense of being unique or different from others.

sentiment socialization Learning how to express emotions and to read others' emotional displays accurately.

sense of constraint A feeling of unease or disempowerment, which working-class children may be socialized to feel in relation to certain important institutions, such as schools and future workplaces.

sense of entitlement A sense of control a child may have over her/his destiny, which is often the product of middle-class socialization. This can imbue a child's life and have a strong effect on her/his future.

sex Biological maleness or femaleness; anatomical and biological phenomena associated with reproduction.

sex chromosomes Genetically encoded information that governs physical and sexual development.

sex hormones Hormones (estrogen, testosterone, progesterone) which govern sexual development (puberty) and reproduction.

sexting A term created by combining the terms "sex" and "texting," referring to the sending photographs or messages of a sexual nature between mobile phones.

sexual ambiguity Biological conditions that make it difficult to determine whether an individual is male or female.

sexual orientation Identifying oneself as heterosexual, bisexual, homosexual, or asexual.

social class Categories of people who occupy similar positions of power or privilege in a society.

social construction The idea that members of a society discover and reaffirm to one another a collective version of the "truth," which they then share; a collective version of knowledge constructed by a group or society.

social control   Laws and norms that limit or constrain individual agency within a society.

social structure   The ways in which society guides individuals' actions to produce patterned behaviors and interactions, including norms and social institutions.

socialization   The process of learning how to act according to the rules of society; the process by which individuals learn to be functioning members of society.

strain theory   A theory developed by sociologist Robert Merton to refer to the disjuncture between the goals people are encouraged by society to achieve and the actual access they have to the *means* of achieving those goals.

subcultures   Groups that are distinguished from the larger culture by different values and behaviors.

tool kit   A collection of resources that humans actors can use for shaping their strategies for action.

total institution   A place where a large number of like-situated individuals, cut off from the wider society for an appreciable period of time, live and work together in an enclosed and formally administered environment.

transitional learning (rehearsal) period   A period in which adults in a child's environment become stand-ins for those they will meet in the future.

transmission of differential advantages   The process through which middle-class parents transmit to middle-class children the social skills through which they can cultivate social capital for the future.

values   Standards people use to decide on desirable goals or courses of action.

vegan   A form of vegetarianism in which an individual consumes no food or dairy products derived from animals and refrains from using animal byproducts.

voluntary resocialization   A form of resocialization in which individuals take on new roles of their own volition or free will.

BIBLIOGRAPHY

Aday, David P. *Social Control at the Margins*. Belmont, Calif.: Wadsworth, 1990.

Adler, Patricia A., and Peter Adler. *Peer Power: Preadolescent Culture and Identity*. New Brunswick, N.J.: Rutgers University Press, 1998.

Berrey, Stephen A. "Resistance begins at home: The black family and lessons in survival and subversion in Jim Crow Mississippi." *Black Women, Gender and Families* 3 (2009): 65–90.

Calzo, Jerel P., and Monique L. Ward. "Contributions of parents, peers, and media to attitudes toward homosexuality: Investigating sex and ethnic differences." *Journal of Homosexuality* 56 (2009): 1101–1116.

Clark, K.B. *The Dark Ghetto: Dilemmas of Social Power*. New York: Harper, 1965.

Collins, Patricia Hill. *Black Feminist Thought: Knowledge, Consciousness and the Politics of Empowerment*. New York: Routledge, 2000.

Cooley, Charles H. *Human Nature and Social Order*. New York: Scribner's, 1902.

Corsaro, William. *The Sociology of Childhood*. Thousand Oaks, Calif.: Pine Forge Press, 1997.

Curra, John O. *The Relativity of Deviance*. Thousand Oaks, Calif.: Pine Forge Press, 2000.

Denzin, Norman K. *Childhood Socialization*. New Brunswick, N.J.: Transaction Publishers, 2010.

Doucet, Andrea. *Do Men Mother? Fathering, Care, and Domestic Responsibility*. Toronto: University of Toronto Press. 2006.

Edelman, Marian Wright. *The Sea Is so Wide and My Boat Is so Small: Charting a Course for the Next Generation.* New York: Hyperion Press, 2008.

Erikson, Kai T. *Wayward Puritans: A Study in the Sociology of Deviance.* New York: Allyn & Bacon, 2004.

Ferguson, Ann. *Bad Boys: Public Schools in the Making of Black Masculinity.* Ann Arbor: University of Michigan Press, 2001.

Goffman, Erving. *Asylums: Essays on the Social Situation of Mental Patients and Other Inmates.* Chicago: Aldine, 1962.

Grusec, Joan E., and Paul D. Hastings (Eds). *Handbook of Socialization: Theory and Research.* New York: The Guilford Press, 2007.

Handel, Gerald, Spencer E. Cahill, and Frederick Elkin. *Children and Society: The Sociology of Children and Childhood Socialization.* Los Angeles, Calif.: Roxbury Publishing, 2007.

Hart, Betty, and Todd Risley. "The early catastrophe: The 30 million word gap." *American Educator* 27 (2003): 4–9.

Hays, Sharon. *The Cultural Contradictions of Motherhood.* New Haven: Yale University Press. 1996.

Hesse-Biber, Sharlene Nagy. *The Cult of Thinness.* New York: Oxford University Press, 2007.

Kimmel, Michael. *The Gendered Society.* New York: Oxford University Press, 2011.

Lareau, Annette. *Unequal Childhoods: Class, Race, and Family Life.* Berkeley, Calif.: University of California Press, 2003.

Lareau, Annette. *Home Advantage: Social Class and Parental Intervention in Elementary Education,* 2nd ed. Lanham, Md.: Rowman & Littlefield 2009,

Laub, John H., and Robert J. Sampson. *Shared Beginnings, Divergent Lives: Delinquent Boys to Age 70.* Cambridge, Mass: Harvard University Press, 2003.

Lee, Shayne. "The church of faith and freedom: African-American Baptists and social action." *Journal for the Scientific Study of Religion* 42 (2003): 31–42.

Martin, Karin A. "'William Wants a Doll. Can He Have One?' Feminists, Child Care Advisors, and Gender-Neutral Child Rearing." *Gender & Society* 19 (2005): 456–479.

Mead, George Herbert. *Mind, Self, & Society.* Chicago: University of Chicago Press, 1934.

Messner, Michael A. *Taking the Field: Women, Men, and Sports.* Minneapolis: University of Minnesota Press, 2002.

Milkie, Melissa A. "Social comparisons, reflected appraisals, and mass media: The impact of pervasive beauty images on black and white girls' self-concepts." *Social Psychology Quarterly* 62 (1999): 190–210.

Newton, Michael. *Savage Girls and Wild Boys: A History of Feral Children.* New York: St. Martin's, 2002.

Pascoe, C.J. *Dude, You're a Fag: Masculinity and Sexuality in High School.* Berkeley, Calif.: University of California Press, 2007.

Reddy, Maureen T. *Crossing the Color Line: Race, Parenting, and Culture.* New Brunswick, N.J.: Rutgers University Press, 1994.

Risman, Barbara J. "College women and sororities: The social construction and reaffirmation of gender roles." *Journal of Contemporary Ethnography* 11 (1982): 231–252.

Spitz, Robert Stephen. *Barefoot in Babylon: The Creation of the Woodstock Music Festival, 1969.* New York: W.W. Norton, 1989.

Saracho, Olivia N., and Bernard Spodek (Eds). *Contemporary Perspectives on Socialization and Social Development in Early Childhood Education.* Charlotte, N.C.: Information Age Publishing, 2007.

Thorne, Barrie. *Gender Play: Girls and Boys in School.* New Brunswick, N.J.: Rutgers University Press, 1999.

Wood, Robert. "Samurai baseball." *Source*: http://www.camden.rutgers.edu/~wood/Video/vt-baseball.htm

INDEX

Index note: Page numbers followed by *g* indicate glossary entries.